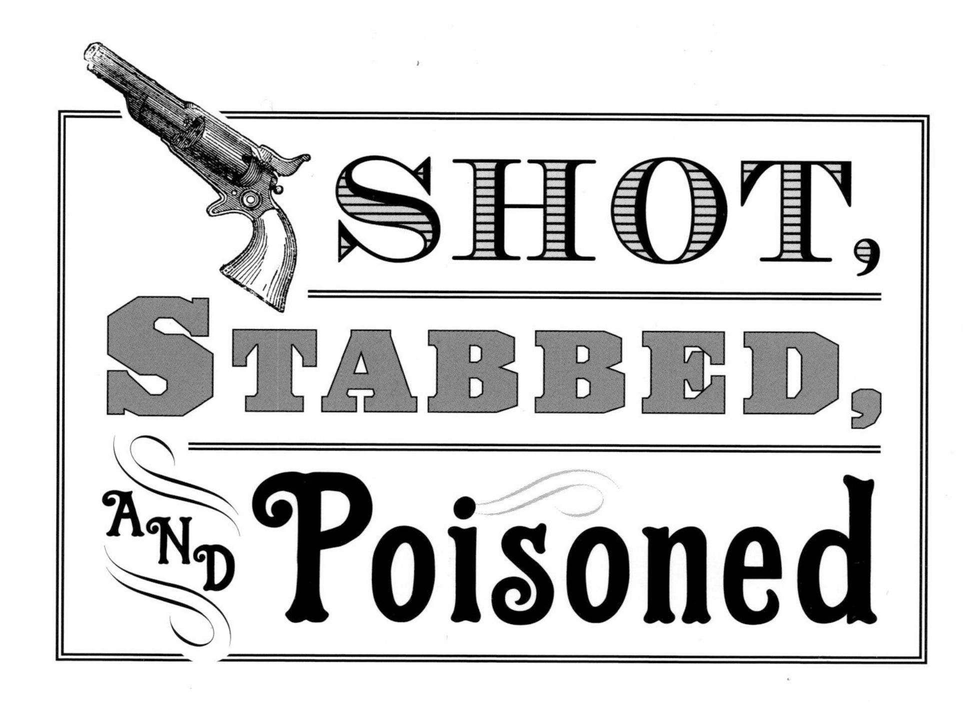
SHOT,
STABBED,
AND Poisoned

An Imprint of Sterling Publishing Co., Inc.
1166 Avenue of the Americas
New York, NY 10036

ISBN 978-1-4351-6764-3

For information about custom editions, special sales, and premium and corporate purchases, please contact Sterling Special Sales at 800-805-5489 or specialsales@sterlingpublishing.com.

Manufactured in China

2 4 6 8 10 9 7 5 3 1

www.sterlingpublishing.com

Credit: Design by Lindsey Johns

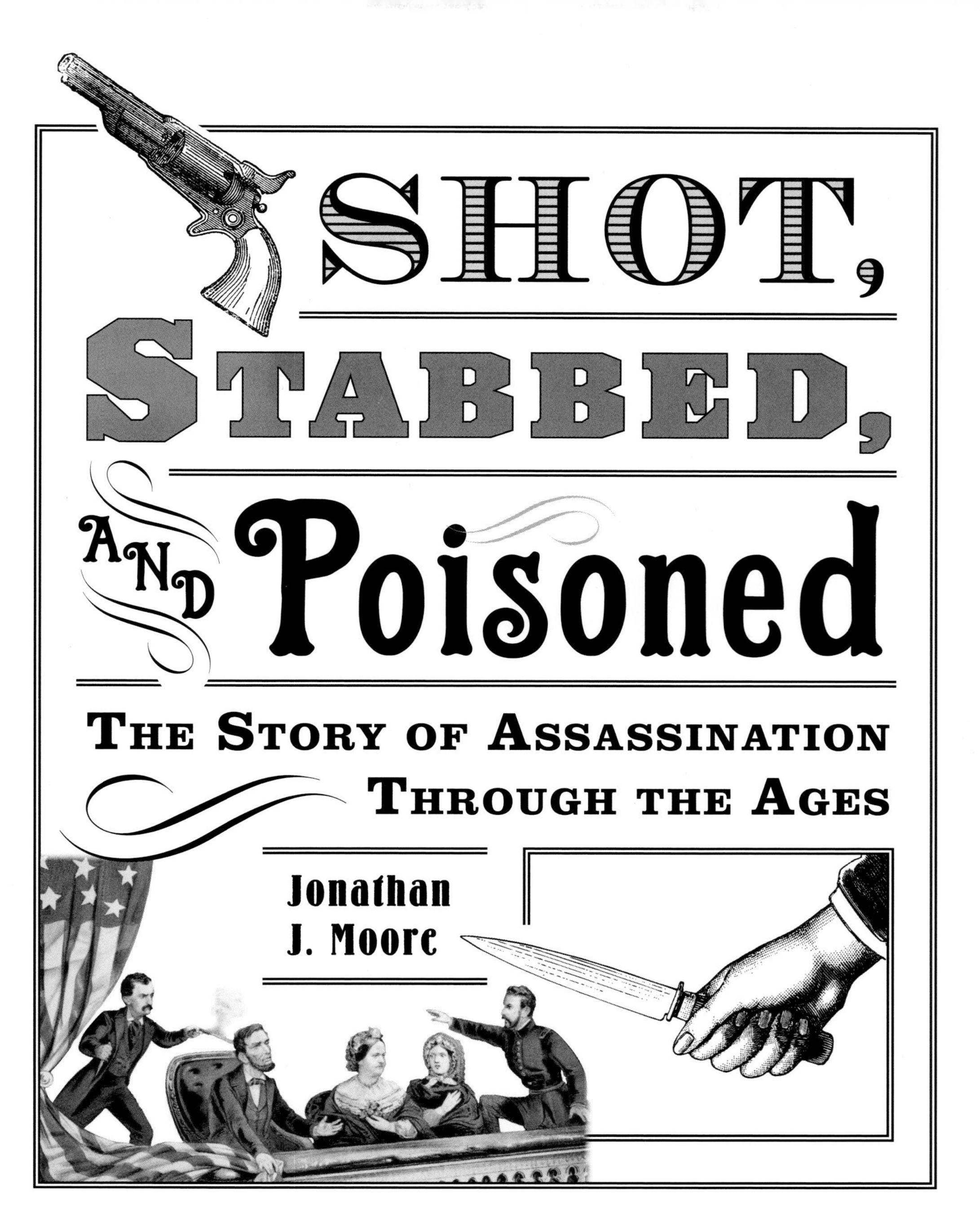

METRO BOOKS
NEW YORK

CONTENTS

CHAPTER
5

CHAPTER
6

CHAPTER
7

À MARAT,
DAVID

INTRODUCTION

IF PROSTITUTION IS THE OLDEST PROFESSION IN THE WORLD, assassination is the second oldest. As soon as hierarchies evolved, leaders who controlled wealth had to protect themselves from usurpers who would seek to gain that wealth for their own designs.

There are many different dictionary definitions of assassination, but they all involve the planned murder of a victim, usually somebody with a high profile, for political or social gain. Treachery and the employment of sudden violence or secret poisoning are often characteristics of this kind of killing. Synonyms include: murder, slaughter, butchery, homicide, liquidation, termination, slaying, "carrying out a hit," and elimination.

EARLY ASSASSINATIONS

The earliest recorded assassination in the Western world is that of Agamemnon, written in Homer's *Odyssey*. The Mycenaean king returned from ten years of fighting before the walls of Troy. He was expecting a warm welcome from his wife, Clytemnestra. The welcome was warmer than he intended. After a good soaking in a bath to wash away the rigors of the campaign, he stepped out into the embrace of his wife, who wrapped a towel around his torso. This served to pin his arms, and the queen's lover, Aegisthus, leapt upon the defenseless Agamemnon and stabbed him to death.

Another assassination occurred at about the same time, more than 3,000 years ago. Remarkably for an event that took place so long ago, we have solid proof that it happened. Ramses III was killed with a knife that slashed his throat from ear to ear. His corpse still exists, and scans have revealed the horrendous wound that ended his life. Thirty-two conspirators were sentenced to

LEFT **Charlotte Corday thought that assassinating Marat would limit French Revolutionary violence. It made it worse, as thousands fell to the guillotine.**

ABOVE **The warrior pharaoh, Ramses III. He fell to an assassin's knife that cut through his throat with such savagery that he was almost decapitated.**

varying forms of punishment after the assassination, and the wounds inflicted upon Ramses' body indicate that more than one assassin attacked him. His throat was gashed with a ghastly 2¾-inch (7-centimeter)-wide wound that penetrated deep enough to damage one of the vertebrae of the royal neck. A toe was chopped off, indicating a ferocious melee that involved several of his guards, one wielding an axe. The last word that Ramses gasped as he bled out could have been "Revenge," for that is what happened.

The chiefs of the chamber, the butlers, the harem, the king's scribe, the palace major-domo, and the commander of the elite Libyan archers were among those tried and sentenced for their part in the conspiracy. Some were executed, others made to commit suicide before the court. The worst fate was perhaps reserved for Ramses' errant son, Pentaweret. In 1881, father and son were found buried together, but rather than being embalmed and preserved as befitted a prince of the royal blood, Pentaweret's corpse was wrapped in an uncured goat's skin. His internal organs were not removed, and he was buried in a plain wooden sarcophagus. The accounts from Egypt indicate that he was either buried alive or strangled. An autopsy of the corpse buried next to Ramses, genetically linked to him through DNA testing, indicated that his neck muscles were constricted enough to cause strangulation. A scan of his lungs showed that they were distended and swollen, a common occurrence with victims of strangulation. Pentaweret paid the price for assassinating his father.

This assassination of the mighty Ramses follows a pattern common for assassinations through the ages. A powerful figure rises within society and attracts the ire or envy of other individuals. Through good fortune or effective planning, these individuals manage to carry out an extra-judicial killing. The assassins usually suffer a horrific fate when a bloody revenge is extracted on their frail flesh.

The Whys and Wherefores

While there have been thousands of assassinations in history, this book addresses the most interesting, gruesome, and earthshaking historical murders. There are many types and targets of assassination. The most obvious targets are Royals and Rulers, who can earn the enmity of their entire kingdoms. Their deaths are often the result of "an inside job" carried out by those who are closest to the target and have the most opportunities—and the most to gain. The Rebels and Revolutionaries are discussed. They are most often targeted by individuals who want to maintain the status quo, not challenge it. Then there are the hard cases whose very foul existence on Earth seems to call for them to be eliminated, the crooks and the evil dictators who spread only death and pain wherever they go. Celebrities are often a target. This seems to be due to their tendency to attract deranged assassins who operate without coherent reason and are motivated by delusional dreams. Perhaps the greatest

BELOW **John Wilkes Booth takes out President Lincoln. The Civil War had ended, but Booth was out to avenge the South's loss.**

assassins are those who operate in the shadow of organized crime. While this book discusses some high-profile Mafia killings, they are only the tip of the proverbial iceberg. Thousands of Made Men and associates have disappeared, never to be seen again. Just as the fate of these unfortunate individuals remains a mystery, their killers are usually unknown except for a small circle of mob enforcers. Finally, we look at those who escaped—the near misses of history.

ABOVE **The Austrian Emperor Franz Joseph survived this assassination attempt in 1853. His heir, Franz Ferdinand, fell to the assassin's bullet in 1914.**

LEFT **Archimedes was the inventor of the first weapons of mass destruction. His brilliant mind couldn't protect him from a Roman soldier's sword.**

The repercussions of these tragic tales can be earth-shattering. The death of Franz Ferdinand led to the two World Wars of the twentieth century, the rise of communism, and perhaps even the terrible threat of nuclear holocaust. Other assassinations led to more localized but still horrific outcomes—thousands of Czechs suffered torture and execution at the hands of outraged Nazis after the attack on Reinhard Heydrich, while Yitzhak Rabin's murder by a fanatic Zionist halted the Arab–Israeli peace process, and even now we are living with the consequences.

Some assassinations, however, cause barely a ripple. Mafia hits, while gruesome, are often just a form of "early retirement" to allow a younger mobster to take over an existing criminal network.

Of course, the other figures in this book are the assassins themselves. In this dicey dance of death, most were seized just after the deadly deed. Their fates reflect the times they lived in. Mark David Chapman, the deranged individual who killed John Lennon, still rots in confinement as he serves a life sentence. Assassins from earlier periods were usually much less fortunate. The killer of Henry IV of France, François Ravaillac, was subjected to prolonged torture before he was torn apart by four horses.

Do the punishments meted out to many assassins fit the crime? You decide.

Royals and Rulers

Without democratic institutions, political power is usually taken by force. As Mao Zedong said: "Political power grows out of the barrel of a gun." It requires continued military or security strength to maintain this power. A royal must always be on guard lest they are attacked. The following rulers, from Philip II of Macedon to Archduke Franz Ferdinand, let their security slip for only a moment, allowing the assassins' knives, bombs, or bullets to do their deadly work.

THE IDES OF MARCH

If you visit the Roman Forum at the dead of night, the ancient ruins of long gone temples and sacred sites seem dusty relics of past glories, old and dead. Doors are closed, and windows are dark; marble ages quietly around you. But in the center of the Forum, under an ancient crumbling platform, a flickering light may be discerned. On approaching the light, you can see that behind the foundations of an ancient altar, there is a small pile of flowers, some coins, and one or two guttering candles. This site is an ancient remnant of the temple built to deify Julius Caesar. More than 2,000 years after his assassination, people still make offerings to this giant of ancient history. It was at this very spot that he was cremated by an outraged mob after his assassination.

Born on July 13, 100 BCE, Caesar was heir to an ancient family who traced their roots back to the mythical founding of Rome. An early career as an adventurer and soldier culminated in his brilliant campaigns from 58 BCE to 50 BCE, in which he conquered much of Gaul (modern-day France and Belgium),

BELOW **The Roman Forum. It was here that Caesar's temple was built on the site of his cremation. Offerings are still made to the "Dictator."**

fought off several German tribes, and even launched a short-lived invasion of the British Isles. He was appointed dictator in 48 BCE. At the time, the term "dictator" did not have the negative connotations associated with it today; the Roman Republic had often appointed dictators at times of crisis. He set about cementing his popular support by a range of measures. He offered gladiatorial games and banquets, built a public library, increased the grain dole to the urban poor, allowed debtors to reduce their debt, brought law and order to the streets of Rome, and embarked on massive building schemes that employed huge numbers of Romans with profitable contracts and well-paying jobs. Eighty thousand landless plebeians (lower-class citizens) were given land grants in captured provinces and encouraged to migrate to fresh pastures.

But while this largesse built Caesar support within some groups, others were alarmed. His conquered territories were assimilated into the Republic, and foreigners were given full Roman citizenship and allowed to join the equites, the upper class of society just below the Senate and an important stepping stone for those who wanted to rise within Roman society. Roman equites and high-born supporters from Gaul were encouraged to join the Senate, and its number was increased from 600 to 900. He had also demonstrated that he could be ruthless: whole tribes—at least 2 million people—had been destroyed in the various campaigns. All the signs were that the dictator was in real terms becoming a king. Rome had a proud reputation for

BELOW Caesar proved unbeatable on the battlefield. Here he accepts the surrender of Vercingetorix at the Siege of Alesia in 52 BCE.

kicking out kings and founding a true democratic republic. By early 44 BCE, Caesar's domination of the Senate ensured that he was proclaimed *Dictator perpetuo*—Dictator for life. Every senator was pressured or willingly swore that they considered Caesar's person sacrosanct, while any who threatened him would earn the death penalty. Just like Philip of Macedon and Alexander the Great before him (see page 23), Caesar was showing a dangerous level of hubris.

ABOVE **Gladiators salute a Roman Emperor. Caesar and his successors won the support of the Roman population with increasingly violent and expensive gladiatorial games.**

This all came to a head in 44 BCE. The Senate proclaimed that Caesar was an official god of the Roman pantheon. He was to have his own temple complete with priests, acolytes, and golden statues. It seems that at this time, Caesar's usual good judgment was evading him. It is possible that due to overwork, he suffered epileptic fits or even mini-strokes. In early 44 BCE, he made a misjudgment and alienated many in the Senate by refusing to rise and greet an official delegation. At the same time, he infringed on the powers of the tribunes— the representatives of the people.

Some powerful Romans decided it was time for Caesar to go, and around February 44 BCE, a plot was hatched to kill him. Cassius (Gaius Cassius Longinus), Brutus (Marcus Junius Brutus), and Decimus (Decimus Junius Brutus Albinus) were outwardly all Caesar's men, but inwardly they were determined to destroy him. Their avowed reason for their actions was to bring down a dictator and re-establish the Republic, but their true motivations were a mix of greed, envy, or thirst for revenge. The conspirators managed to assemble approximately 60 like-minded senators, and plans for Caesar's assassination were made.

ABOVE **The Republic of Rome nestled in the bend of the Tiber River. Fears of a dictatorship led to Caesar's assassination.**

The plotters knew that Caesar was a hard target to reach—Rome was almost more of an armed camp than a civilian city in peacetime. A short distance away, on the Tiber Island, the bulk of a legion loyal to the dictator was encamped. Throughout the city, thousands of demobilized legionaries were awaiting the time when they would be led out to settle the agricultural plots that Caesar had granted them on cessation of their service. Many were flush with funds, all due to the generosity of their former commander. When touring the countryside, Caesar had a permanent detachment, at least 2,000 strong, drawn from his legions. While moving about the city, he was borne on a palanquin (litter) carried by burly slaves, and he was always surrounded by 24 lictors, ex-soldiers armed with the fasces—axes bound with rods. While these were ceremonial, they could be turned into deadly weapons if needed. What's more, as the dispenser of favors and positions within the Republic, Caesar was perpetually surrounded by a flock of adherents and supporters, determined to protect their patron.

There was one place that this retinue could not follow Caesar: an assembly of the Senate. Only senators and a small, select group of secretaries were allowed on the premises. The sacred laws of the Senate would have guaranteed his safety there—if they were followed. It was an offense to carry weapons or commit any acts of violence within any of the Senate precincts. The conspirators decided to break this law. They were, after all, assassinating a dictator to protect their sacred Republic. Surely justice was on their side?

There were other advantages, too. Senators wore the traditional toga, a voluminous robe that was swathed in layers around the body. Beneath the toga, they wore a belt, the perfect location to secrete their daggers. The conspiratorial senators met at the Curia Julia (the Senate House) in the Theatre of Pompey. The assassination was planned to operate like a military operation. About 20 to 30 conspirators were detailed to kill the tyrant while the other half surrounded the attackers, facing outward, ready to repel any of Caesar's adherents who sought to interfere with the violent deed. Boxes of parchments and official records delivered to the Senate were heavier than usual—they had been filled with weapons for the conspirators to use if needed. As final backup, Decimus brought several hundred of his trained gladiators. They were exercising in the Theatre of Pompey and could be called upon if necessary.

On the morning of March 14, 44 BCE, Caesar was due to visit the Senate. It was to be his last hearing before he embarked on a war against the Parthians in the east of the empire. The conspirators had to strike; it might be the last chance they had.

But while the senators waited anxiously for several hours, it appeared their well-laid plans might come to naught. The combination of a succession of bad omens and his wife's entreaties (see box on page 21), as well as an upset stomach from overindulgence at a banquet put on by his ally Lepidus the previous night, had prompted Caesar to send one of his key supporters, Mark Antony, in his stead. Once they heard this, the three chief conspirators resolved to send Decimus to change his mind. Caesar and Decimus had fought many a battle, some on the same side but others as enemies. Decimus used the language of battle to shame Caesar out of his funk, questioning whether it was worthy of such a great man to listen to the entreaties of a woman and an Etruscan priest.

BELOW **Cicero was one of Caesar's fiercest critics. He paid for his part in the assassination by having his head and right hand cut off.**

Caesar was convinced. He summoned his palanquin and slaves, and proceeded to the Theatre of Pompey. Even on the way to the Senate, surrounded by his lictors, it is possible that Caesar may have escaped the assassins. Artemidorus of Cnidos, to whose father Caesar had granted freedom of the city, approached Caesar's litter and pressed into his hand a small scroll warning of the conspiracy, urging him to read it immediately. But Caesar did not have a chance to, and he died with it still clutched in his hand.

By 11:30, he had arrived at his destination. Once again, mutterings and rumors were heard that should have alarmed the target of the assassins' wrath. But Decimus was on hand to encourage his mark over the threshold.

There were at least 200 senators in the room, and they rose to greet their leader. Mark Antony did not accompany his patron; the plotters detailed a comrade to keep him talking outside. As Caesar approached the dais and his golden chair, the conspirators surrounded him, fawning and paying him compliments. As he sat down, one of his veteran soldiers, Tillius Cimber, approached. Well trusted by Caesar, Cimber presented a petition on behalf of his exiled half-brother before grabbing the hems of Caesar's toga and pinning him to his chair. This would have been the first intimation that all was not well…

Others grabbed the dictator's arms, holding him down. While he was held, pinioned and helpless like a sacrificial animal, the conspirators drew their leaf-shaped military daggers from beneath their togas

LEFT **Julius Caesar at first heeded the warnings of his wife Calpurnia, but then listened to Decimus, with fatal consequences.**

BELOW **A well-planned attack. While some senators pinned Caesar to the rostrum, others drew their daggers and repeatedly stabbed him.**

and set upon Caesar. Servilius Casca was the first to strike the dictator, aiming at his neck with a downward thrust. Caesar struggled, and the potentially mortal thrust merely inflicted a flesh wound on his chest. The conspirators' target managed to free himself and stood up, thrusting Casca away and perhaps jabbing him in the eye with a stylus. Casca called for aid from his brother, and Gaius Casca thrust his dagger into Caesar's ribcage.

He continued to struggle but it was too late. The conspirators swarmed over Caesar, and the blows from up to 20 daggers landed thick and fast on the struggling Roman. Such was the mayhem that even some of the conspirators were struck; one was hit in the thigh, and Brutus was stabbed in the hand. It is unlikely that the Shakespearian line "Et tu, Brute?" was really uttered in the melee but was later introduced into the narrative for dramatic effect. What does seem to have happened is that, as his life blood drained from him, Caesar slumped to the floor, simultaneously covering his face with his toga, for protection or in shame.

Caesar's death had several consequences. In the short term, it sparked another round of civil wars that did not come to an end until his heir, Octavian, defeated Mark Antony in 30 BCE. He was later proclaimed Augustus Caesar, who is considered the first Roman emperor. This sounded the death knell of the Republic, and Rome was ruled evermore by a succession of emperors.

BELOW The assassins celebrate by waving their bloody daggers in the air. Few would survive the revenge of Marc Antony in the civil war that followed.

Supernatural Forewarning

According to various ancient writers, it seems that the entire universe was warning Caesar not to attend the Senate on that fateful sitting on March 15, 44 BCE. For months, Romans throughout the empire had been reporting strange and alarming omens. Birds had dropped from the sky, men had burst into flame, weird lights were seen around the Capitol, weapons had disintegrated, and horses that had borne Caesar across the Rubicon had begun to shed tears. Most remarkable was the sighting of a wren carrying a laurel branch (Caesar had worn laurel wreaths at all of his previous triumphs) that flew into the Senate building, where it was torn apart by a flock of assorted birds.

More alarming was the prophecy of the Etruscan soothsayer Spurinna. On February 15, he had sacrificed a bull in Caesar's honor at the festival of Lupercalia. What Spurinna found that day shocked him: The bull lacked a heart. The following day, another sacrifice revealed a diseased liver. The soothsayer interpreted the signs and declared to his patron that he must be alert to danger in the 30 days before March 15, the oft quoted "Ides of March."

His wife, Calpurnia, had been unsettled for several weeks, plagued by nightmares and foreboding. On the night of March 14/15, these dreams had intensified, and she was jolted awake by the horrific nightmare of holding her husband dead in her arms.

By the morning of March 15, these warnings had finally got through to the dictator. No doubt trying to cheer himself up, he said to Spurinna, "The Ides of March have come." Spurinna shot back: "They have come, but not yet passed."

RIGHT **Caesar is still seen as one of the greatest commanders in history.**

The Violent Fate of Roman Emperors

The Julio-Claudian line (14–68 CE) had its fair share of assassinations, but they at least enjoyed some years of power—not all were so lucky.

Caligula (r. March 37–January 41 CE) was hacked to pieces and gutted by the Praetorian Guard in a corridor of his palace. His infant daughter had her head smashed against the corridor wall.

Claudius (r. January 41–October 54 CE) loved mushrooms so much that his wife was able to slip some poisonous toadstools into his soup.

Galba (r. June 68–January 69 CE) had been an emperor for only a few months when he was hacked to pieces by the Praetorian Guard in the Roman Forum. His head was presented to his successor, Otho.

Vitellius (r. April–December 69 CE) succeeded Otho, but only for a short time. Vespasian's troopers tortured and dismembered the emperor and threw his corpse in the Tiber.

Domitian (r. September 81–September 96 CE) alienated everybody, including his wife and the Praetorian Guard. It fell to an ex-slave, Stephanus, to kill the demented emperor by stabbing him repeatedly in the groin.

Commodus (r. 177–December 192 CE), a debauched megalomaniac, ended a golden age of stable Roman rule during the 2nd century CE. He was drowned in his bath by a gladiator, Narcissus.

Pertinax (r. January–March 193 CE) tried to appeal to the Praetorians' democratic instincts and promptly received a javelin in his chest for his troubles.

Julianus (r. March–June 193 CE) purchased the throne on the death of Pertinax but the Senate hired an assassin who killed him soon after.

Pescennius Niger (r. April 193–May 194 CE) lost a battle and lost his life when his defeated soldiers turned on him.

Geta (r. 209–December 211 CE) was co-emperor with his older brother Caracalla. He was hacked to death by the Praetorian Guard and died in his mother's arms.

Caracalla (r. 198–April 217 CE) descended from his carriage while on the march in Syria to urinate by the side of the road, only to be stabbed in the side by an agent sent by his Praetorian Prefect.

THE CONSEQUENCES OF HUBRIS

Few men can be credited with changing world history, but King Philip II of Macedon was one of these rare individuals. He turned a ragtag mountain kingdom of herders and farmers into one of the first modern nation states. During this time, he forged a new and unbeatable army. When Philip was assassinated, his dynamic son, Alexander the Great (356–323 BCE), became the Macedonian king and embarked upon a career of conquest almost unparalleled in the course of history. The Hellenistic way of life was spread through much of the East before being adopted by the Romans, and hence on to Europe and the world.

But even through the mists of time, there are suspicions that in fact Alexander was responsible for his father's death. If it were not for the assassination, maybe the most famous general in history would be called "Philip the Great."

As a youth, Philip of Macedon (b. c.383 BCE) was held hostage in the Theban court, the most powerful Greek city-state at the time; but as a noble, he was educated while there, tutored by the great military innovator Epaminondas (c.420–362 BCE). A spark of genius was in Philip's soul and, determined to make Macedon a great power once he assumed the throne in 359 BCE, he reflected on the lessons learned from the Battle of Leuctra (371 BCE), where Greek spearmen (hoplites) were amassed in deep formations,

BELOW Phillip II of Macedon developed the phalanx of pike-armed Phalangites. This formation ruled the battlefield until defeat by the Roman legions.

to revolutionize warfare and create an entirely new style of army. He not only placed his men in deep formations but equipped them with a new deadly weapon known as the sarissa (an extraordinarily long spear).

After securing his borders and putting down troublesome tribes around the periphery of his Macedonian kingdom, Philip resolved to embark on his next major scheme, the conquest of the Persian Empire. But he needed the support of the other Greek city-states, so in 358 BCE he began his campaign for supremacy and soon occupied much of northern Greece, as well as Thrace. Any who were unwilling to join him were shown the error of their ways by defeat in battle.

In 338 BCE, concerned with Philip's increasing power on the mainland, Thebes and Athens united to fight him. They were defeated at the Battle of Chaeronea, where the Macedonian phalanx fixed the allied Greek hoplites in place before Alexander, at the head of his unit, launched a devastating attack into their flank. The "Sacred Band," made up of the cream of Theban youth, was killed to a man, and as the rest of the allied forces fled, there was no longer any state that could oppose Macedonian hegemony in Greece.

All the pieces for Philip's attack on Persia were in place. He organized the League of Corinth (the Hellenic League) in 337 BCE and enrolled all the conquered Greek states. He became the hegemon (leader) and had begun his attack toward the Achaemenids when, in October 336 BCE, he was assassinated in the Theatre of Aegae by one of his bodyguards, Pausanias. The Greeks have a term, "hubris," which means that if a human behaves in such an arrogant manner that they seek to rival the gods in greatness, they will be brought down.

Philip displayed hubris on the day of his assassination. Despite the fact that he was a grizzled veteran of countless combats and battles (he had lost an eye to a sword stroke years earlier and had a knee all but destroyed by a Scythian lance), he abandoned basic security. Believing that he was supreme in Greece and Macedonia, Philip arranged the marriage of one of his daughters to a client king. Well-wishers were invited from all over

LEFT **Philip II of Macedon was a military innovator and ruthless fighter who laid the foundations of Alexander the Great's success.**

RIGHT **Philip followed statues of the Gods into the theater after leaving his guards behind. Pausanius's dagger proved that the king was no immortal.**

Greece, and several days of feasting and gift-giving were to culminate in a tremendous procession ending in the Theatre of Aegae. The centerpiece of the procession comprised twelve gorgeous statues of the gods, seated upon thrones and decorated with rich metals and jewels. There was a thirteenth statue, that of Philip himself, enthroned like the gods. Once the theatre was filled with the adoring crowd, Philip made his grand entrance. Once again, feeling that his position was secure and placing himself well above the common ruck, he entered unarmed and unguarded. Philip had ordered his personal guards to stay well away. Some were ordered to precede him and some to follow, but they were to keep their distance.

The Bones Tell a Story

In an amazing development, Philip's tomb was discovered in 1977 in Vergina, northern Greece. The skeleton of a 45-year-old man was excavated, and it fitted the description of Philip II to a tee. Not only did the skull reveal a sword cut that would have taken out his right eye, but his left leg showed tremendous damage from a war wound. Some signs that could be interpreted as a wound located near his ribs were found, although the bone was not nicked, proving that Pausanias aimed true.

BELOW Remarkably, the tomb of Philip II was discovered in Vergina, Macedonia. His bones were preserved in this gold coffin.

...AS PAUSANIAS RAN AT HIS HORSE HE CAUGHT HIS SANDAL ON A VINE AND TRIPPED HEAD OVER HEELS. THE THREE BODYGUARDS WERE UPON HIM AND, AS HE ROSE, PERDICCAS AND ATTALUS GRABBED HIM WHILE LEONNATUS RAN HIM THROUGH WITH HIS SPEAR.

A Macedonian member of Philip's guard took the opportunity to strike. Pausanias had planned well ahead and concealed a "Celtic" dagger in his robes, while a fast horse was tethered near the theatre's exit. Once he saw the king striding into the theatre alone, Pausanias struck. As a trained Macedonian soldier, he knew exactly how to wield his weapon with deadly efficiency. He flung himself on the king and plunged the dagger between Philip's ribs, killing him immediately.

Pausanias leapt off the king's prostrate form and fled. Three bodyguards, Leonnatus, Perdiccas, and Attalus, pursued the assassin. It seemed that all was lost and he would escape on horseback, but as Pausanias ran at his horse, he caught his sandal on a vine and tripped head over heels. The three bodyguards were upon him and, as he rose, Perdiccas and Attalus grabbed him while Leonnatus ran him through with his spear.

All was chaos in the theatre as bodyguards ran to protect their charges. One client king had the presence of mind to declare allegiance to Philip's son, Alexander III, who in a few short years would be known as Alexander the Great.

BELOW Alexander led the Macedonian army to glory and crushed the Persian Empire. But did he have a hand in his father's death?

ABOVE **This 1474 woodcut shows Philip's wife Olympias, Alexander's mother, executing Pausanias and the king's second wife, Cleopatra.**

Over time, several theories arose as to the motivation for Pausanias's attack on the king. The most common is that he was once Philip's favorite but had fallen out of favor. Thus, jealousy was the key motive. Another is that Pausanias was in the pay of the Persians. Philip was preparing to cross the Bosporus and attack the Achaemenid Empire with his almost invulnerable phalanx.

Or possibly it was a palace coup. Alexander had already proved himself on the battlefield and considered himself ready to rule. If he then suborned Philip's guards to kill Pausanias, they performed the oldest trick in the book. A dead assassin could not be interrogated, nor Alexander's hand in the attack revealed.

Further punishments followed. Pausanias's body was crucified, and his relay of getaway horses were sacrificed as they were also deemed guilty for their part in the king's murder. There was a general purge in the ranks of the Macedonian nobility, with at least ten nobles executed or murdered for any suspected role in the attack. Philip's diviner was crucified for not reading the omens correctly and failing to prophesy that something bad was about to happen!

Whatever the cause of the assassination, the Greeks were unanimous—Philip had died not because of the assassin's blade but because of hubris, putting himself on the same level as the gods.

The Bones in the Lead Casket

King Ethelred (c.968–1016) was directly or indirectly responsible for the murder of his half-brother, King Edward, in 978. While good for Ethelred, who succeeded to the throne, it was a disaster for the Anglo-Saxon inhabitants in England, as it led to decades of Norse invasions, culminating in the Norman conquest of 1066. So bad was his leadership that the new king earned the epithet "Ethelred the Unready."

King Edward (b. 962), also known as Edward the Martyr and Saint Edward, had been king for only three years when he was assassinated, supposedly on the orders of his stepmother, Queen Elfrida, who wanted her natural son, Ethelred, to take the throne. She may not have been alone in her wishes to be rid of the young king, as he had a reputation for random violence, drunkenness, and debauchery. This is perhaps surprising, since his father was King Edgar the Peaceful.

Byrhtferth of Ramsey was a scholarly monk in the king's retinue who witnessed the cold-blooded assassination of his lord. As the royal party left Corfe Castle, Elfrida's home, several members of Ethelred's retinue converged on the king and, while appearing respectful, one noble grabbed the young man's hand and pinioned his arm to his side. Unable to draw his sword, the king cried out in distress words to the effect: "What are you doing, breaking my right arm? Begone." One of the attackers then drew his knife and stabbed the king. Since the king was mounted, the thrust was likely up into his ribcage. The king's horse, panicked by the tumult, reared and smashed the monarch onto the high cantle of the saddle. Although the soldiers sought to hold him down, the king's right leg swept out of the stirrup and was crushed against the cantle and twisted as he fell.

RIGHT **Ethelred the Unready. Another interpretation of his name was Ethelred the Badly Advised. Either way, his rule was disastrous for his kingdom.**

The horse bolted and dragged Edward by his left foot, which was still in the stirrup. With a broken arm, stab wounds, and the shock of being dragged by a bolting charger, the king soon succumbed to his fate.

The king's dubious reputation in life did not follow him in death, and in 1001 he was canonized after those praying at his tomb at Wareham began to claim miraculous interventions. The wealthy Shaftesbury Abbey obtained the royal relics and placed them within a shrine where they became a favored destination for pilgrims right up until the dissolution of the monasteries under the Tudor king Henry VIII (1491–1547). For safe keeping, the remains were then buried in the abbey's grounds, but in 1931 they were dug up again and subjected to forensic analysis. The excavating archaeologist, J. Wilson Claridge, found the lead casket, which was 21 inches (53cm) long, 11 inches (28cm) wide, and 9 inches (23cm) deep. The bones had been carefully and respectfully packed within the casket, and Claridge suspected they may be the remains of the sainted king. He conferred with a forensic pathologist, Thomas E. A. Stowell, who immediately identified a large number of "greenstick fracture" breaks within the bone, sustained by young people when their limbs are subjected to intense violent pressure—perfectly filling the graphic scene painted by Byrhtferth of Ramsey so many years before.

Under further examination, the bones were found to belong to a male between 5 foot 6 (1.68m) and 5 foot 8 (1.72m) in height and somewhere between 17 and 21 years of age. The skull was classified as "long headed," which was the genetic heritage of the Saxons. Other wounds were found. Stowell determined that the youth's neck had been broken and that his right arm had been broken or fractured in at least four places, signs he had seen before on assault victims when their arms are twisted violently behind their back. The conclusive evidence was the left thigh bone, which had suffered a transverse greenstick fracture. Here the bone is split upward and downward, a sign that the body had been dragged by the foot for a considerable distance. Remarkably, Stowell had seen an identical wound several years earlier: The autopsy of a boy who had been dragged along the ground with his foot upward had displayed exactly the same wound.

LEFT **While Queen Elfrida offered wine to her stepson, she had already arranged for a team of assassins to ambush the king as he left her castle.**

THE HORSE BOLTED AND DRAGGED EDWARD BY HIS LEFT FOOT, WHICH WAS STILL IN THE STIRRUP. WITH A BROKEN ARM, STAB WOUNDS, AND THE SHOCK OF BEING DRAGGED BY A BOLTING CHARGER, THE KING SOON SUCCUMBED TO HIS FATE.

The poor king's catalogue of wounds did not end there. The right shoulder blade, right elbow, and right haunch bone displayed wounds consistent with a heavy fall from a height such as a horse's saddle. Stowell was satisfied he had solved the mystery of the bones in the casket and declared that the physical damage exactly matched the description of King Edward's assassination.

There is less of a mystery as to why Edward was sainted. His half-brother's rule was marked by dreadful decisions that saw huge amounts of gold paid to the Danes (Danegeld), repeated invasions, lost battles, massacres, and failed crops.

Death by Red-Hot Poker

Being assassinated would be bad enough, but getting a red-hot poker or a crossbow bolt up your butt would be the worst possible way to go. This was the fate of two English kings—Edmund Ironside (c.990–1016) and Edward II (1284–1327).

Edward II's wife was very angry with him. Queen Isabella was so upset that she raised the flag of rebellion and installed her under-age son, Edward III, on the throne. Poor old Edward II was imprisoned in a draughty cell on the top of the tallest tower of Berkeley Castle in Gloucestershire. But things were going to get a lot worse. It seems that one of the key reasons that Isabella decided she wanted her husband out of the way was his penchant for "passive" buggery—he had a succession of young lovers and rarely performed his "kingly duty" with his wife. It was maybe this that accounted for his particularly grisly death.

On September 21, the new regime's enforcers stormed up to the imprisoned king's cell. He was seized, turned around, and held down on a heavy wooden table. The royal breeches were removed and a red-hot poker was pushed up his anus. This was then thrust back and forth and around

LEFT **Queen Isabella took a horrific revenge on her errant husband. She knew his sexual tastes and devised a unique method of assassination.**

so as to rupture his internal organs and kill him. The king's agonized screams were reported to be heard miles away. No wonder. (Apparently, the ghost of the king can still be seen cowering in his cell by the occasional visitor to Berkeley Castle.)

ABOVE **Edward II of England (1284–1327). His ghost is rumored to haunt the tower of Berkley Castle, England.**

If the story is true, it seems that Isabella came up with the idea so that no external mark would be left on her deceased husband's body, and the new king could say it was a natural death. The fate of the king's favorite lover was not much better. Hugh Despenser was castrated before he was hanged.

ABOVE **Edmund Ironside and Cnut the Great sort out their differences. A short truce followed before Edmund suffered a horrible death.**

Edmund Ironside was the son of King Ethelred the Unready. He was given the rule of Wessex by the Danish king Cnut in October 1016. Cnut was obviously not happy with the way Edmund was ruling and decided to take care of business while Edmund was doing his business. On November 30, 1016, Edmund went to satisfy the call of nature, and while he was at his ease sitting on the privy, the son of an earl, who was hiding in said privy, stabbed him twice in the rear end with a long dagger. Other versions say that a spring-bow—a booby-trapped crossbow—was the lethal weapon employed. Whichever is true, it would be a shocking surprise.

A Royal Contract Killing

The assassination of William I, Prince of Orange (1533–1584), is remarkable for two things. It was the first royal assassination by firearm and the only time a king has put out a contract on a fellow ruler.

William was originally a devoted follower of the Hapsburg emperor Charles V, but when he was placed in charge of the Spanish Netherlands, he became disturbed by the Spanish treatment of Dutch Protestants. He led the United Provinces in what is now known as the Eighty Years' War and was such a thorn in the Spanish side that in 1580 the new Hapsburg ruler, Philip II, issued a contract to kill William and declared him an outlaw. He offered 25,000 guilders for William and described the Protestant prince as a bigamist, a drunkard, and a heretic.

In July 1584, Balthasar Gérard took up the offer and insinuated himself into the prince's company. He pulled two wheel locks on the prince and fired them into his chest. Wheel locks are tricky at the best of times, but Gérard shot true, and bullets smashed through William's chest and lodged in the wall behind him.

Gérard never got to collect his reward. He was arrested, tried, and executed. His right hand was burned off with a red-hot iron, pincers tore flesh from six parts of his body, he was disemboweled, and his heart was flung onto his face. He was then quartered and portions of his body hung from the town gates throughout William's princely domains.

BELOW **William I, Prince of Orange is shot by Balthasar Gérard. The bullets embedded in a wall after they passed through the prince.**

The First Conspiracy Killer

A ruler is being driven through the center of town. He is known as a great leader who symbolizes new hope for the nation. Imbued with charismatic bearing, he is intent on overcoming prejudice and uniting all people within his realm. Then suddenly, out of the blue, a lone killer strikes and inflicts two deadly wounds. The victim is rushed to a hospital, and doctors do all they can but cannot save the ruler's life. The attacker is arrested and killed for the crime. It seems he acted alone, but conspiracy theories soon emerge pointing at powerful forces that planned and carried out the assassination. Sound familiar?

It is not the death of JFK being described here but the killing of Henry IV of France approximately 350 years earlier.

Henry was born on December 13, 1553, and ruled France from 1589 to 1610. He was raised a Protestant but converted to Catholicism later in life. He earned the title "Good King Henry" for his efforts to restore harmony to his kingdom after many years of religious conflict. Henry was no milksop and was a successful military commander and financial reformer. This brought a much-needed stability and prosperity to France. But not all were happy. Many fanatic Catholics resented his even-handed treatment of the Huguenots (French Protestants), and there were at least 20 elaborate assassination attempts on Henry in his lifetime.

On May 14, 1610, Henry's luck ran out. The king and his guards were travelling through the center of Paris in an open carriage. Suddenly their way was impeded by two carts whose traces were snarled together. The royal guards left the carriage and sought to clear the way.

Just at that moment, a lunatic drifter named François Ravaillac drew a long dirk from his dark robes, leapt on to the sideboard, and plunged the dagger under the king's left arm. This was a superficial wound. Ravaillac was something of an athlete; he leapt higher and, with his right foot on the wheel housing, stabbed downward into the left side

LEFT A portrait of the drifter François Ravaillac and his lethal dagger. Did he act alone or was he part of a larger conspiracy?

of the king's chest, tearing open the lungs and leading to rapid bleeding into the chest cavity. He was rushed to the Louvre (still a palace at that time) but little could be done to save the stricken monarch.

ABOVE **Ravaillac leapt upon the royal carriage's wheel and thrust down with his dagger to attack the king. Here he is arrested after mortally wounding Henry.**

Ravaillac was arrested and questioned. His background revealed a difficult past where he often saw visions and raved to himself. The killer had tried to join many religious orders but had been refused by all.

The assassin was repeatedly tortured, but he could not account for his actions and stuck to the line that he was doing God's work to avenge Henry's invasion of the Hapsburg Lowlands. Ravaillac insisted he had acted alone and had no co-conspirators. Even as he was taken to his gruesome death, the mad drifter stuck to his story. The French punishment for regicide was to be torn apart by four horses. The executioner facilitated the process by inserting a knife into the shoulder

and thigh joints to dislocate the limbs. That was not all. Before being drawn and quartered, the assassin was scalded with burning sulfur, molten lead, and boiling oil and resin; then his flesh was torn with pincers.

But soon people began to question the lone assassin theory. The king had just crowned his wife, Marie de' Medici—a member of that most conniving of clans. (The Swiss Guards roasted one of the regicide's quarters under her window!) It also turned out that some in Henry's court knew the killer and had even furnished him with lodgings and cash. Was it a coincidence that the carts had stopped the king's progress at just the right time for Ravaillac to strike? And why had no guards stayed with their sovereign? The mystery remains.

LEFT **Queen Marie de' Medici (1575–1642) came from a long line of ruthless powerbrokers. Did she have a hand in her husband's murder?**

ABOVE **Francois Ravaillac suffers the punishment for the crime of regicide—quartering by four horses.**

GUSTAV'S GRISLY END

Gustav III of Sweden seemed to be a perfect monarch. Cultivated and learned, he brought in many lasting reforms while sponsoring the humanities and the arts within his kingdom. Born in 1746, he ascended the throne of Sweden in 1771.

Once enthroned, the picture was not too rosy. He found himself largely powerless due to the domination of law-making powers by the Swedish nobility in the Riksdag (parliament). They were not, it seems, working toward a stronger Sweden. Factionalism and conflict were rife, while the nobles sought to extend their power and exploit their prerogatives. Some factions were bent on emasculating the Swedish military and even entering into traitorous negotiations with the arch-enemy, Russia.

BELOW **Gustav III, King of Sweden 1772–1792. His reforms alienated many in the Swedish nobility.**

Sweden had a long tradition of kings who were military geniuses. Charles II (1697–1718) fought off a host of enemies in the Great Northern War (1700–1721) and dominated his foes with his small but brilliantly handled army. Gustavus Adolphus (1594–1632) was the preeminent tactician of his day and won notable victories in the Thirty Years' War (1618–48). Gustav was determined to emulate his forbears and, gathering loyal officers around him, he seized power from the parliamentary government in 1772. He reinstated his royal powers over a period of time, and when the Union and Security Act was passed in 1789 it could be truly argued that autocracy had returned to Sweden.

Gustav immediately made his mark as an enlightened despot. Well versed in enlightenment literature, he genuinely tried to improve the existence of his subjects. Torture and capital punishment were limited. Catholic and Jewish inhabitants were given full rights as enjoyed by their Protestant compatriots. As a friend of the arts, Gustav founded the Swedish Academy and the Royal Swedish Opera. The young ruler rewarded excellence in the fields of science, industry, and commerce by founding the Royal Order of Vasa. He amended the

BELOW **King Gustav III of Sweden and his brothers.**

ABOVE At the Battle of Svenskund Gustav proved his ability to command and reinstated Sweden as a power to be reckoned with.

Poor Law and eliminated corruption. The tax burden on peasants was reduced with free trade in grain and the removal of oppressive export tolls. The finances of his kingdom were put in order with the "currency realization ordinance" of 1776.

What's more, he was a charming individual who wrote plays and poetry, and could converse with the most respected individuals in Europe, turning the Swedish Royal Court into a beacon of culture that attracted the brightest and best.

Gustav was also an inspired military commander. His strength of personality allowed him to lead a small group of 200 officers to overthrow the corrupt parliamentary government and force Sweden's nobles to swear a new oath of allegiance. His inspired leadership at the Battle of Svensksund (1789) once again established Sweden as a military power to be reckoned with. Ironically, just as Gustav sought to cobble together a coalition of monarchies to reinstate the French monarchy in revolution-torn France, his own nobles turned on him.

Gustav continued to gather power in his royal hands and even removed his nobles' traditional control of the sale of alcohol. This may have been the straw that broke the camel's back, and in 1792 a small group of determined conspirators decided to assassinate their king.

On the evening of March 16, 1792, the king arrived at the newly built Royal Opera House. The masked ball was one of the highlights of Stockholm society's social calendar. It would be a night to remember. The king looked magnificent in his broad-brimmed hat, cape, and mask. He stood out from the rest by sporting his Royal Order of the Seraphim, a decoration only he could wear.

Before the ball, the king dined with some friends. A letter was passed to him that warned of the conspiracy. Rather than being a vague statement that the king should be on his guard, the content of the letter—later found to be written by the colonel of

the Life Guard Cavalry Regiment, Carl Pontus Lilliehorn—was clear. He was about to be killed during the "damnable ball" by conspirators in disguise. The letter then urged Gustav to cancel the ball.

The king was having none of it, and the ball went ahead. Among the swirling gowns and cloaks, five conspirators surrounded the king. Jacob Johan Anckarström greeted the monarch in French and, taking station behind him, he pulled out a pistol and fired into the left rear side of the royal back. It was a dirty round—rather than a regular charge, Anckarström had the pistol loaded with five nails, two balls, and some shot.

BELOW Anckarstrom never repented his actions, even after horrific torture. His family was stripped of wealth and privileges.

Gustav stayed upright and ordered his guards to arrest the shooter. The faces of Anckarström and his conspirators were, of course, covered with black masks, but as the assassin fled he threw the gun aside. It was retrieved, and the next day a gunsmith was able to reveal its owner. Soon all the conspirators were arrested.

At first it seemed that the king might survive. But the extra materials discharged into his back did their deadly work, and the wound soon turned septic. Gustav died on March 29.

Anckarström felt the full power of the law. He was stripped of all his titles, and his property was seized by the crown. He was flogged while suspended from a pole in chains before his right hand was cut off. After the wound was cauterized to prevent death through blood loss, the assassin was quartered while still alive, and finally his head was cut off. He impressed all with his bravery and went to his death expressing the "utmost satisfaction" that he had killed the tyrant.

Gustav's heir, Gustav IV, ruled until 1809, when he was successfully forced from the throne by the very nobles his father had sought to control.

LEFT The king was shot in the back at a masked ball. His attackers recognized him by the Royal Order of Seraphim worn on his chest.

A Mad Tyrant

Every dynasty has to have at least one mad tyrant tucked away in the family tree. The Romanovs had Paul I. During his short reign, he managed to alienate almost every group in Russian society and his death was greeted with celebrations and fireworks.

From an early age, Paul I (b. 1754) enjoyed drilling troops and designing uniforms. He had a great love for all things Prussian and a hatred for all things French. As soon as Paul became ruler in 1796, he sought to turn back the clock. New Prussian-style uniforms were introduced, as was a new military drill manual that reintroduced a strict discipline and drill based on the Prussian model, which sought to enforce correct behavior through violence. Even the slightest error in drill could lead to harsh punishment for enlisted men and officers alike. Three-and-a-half thousand officers, about one-quarter of the entire officer corps, resigned during the mad Czar's rule. Paul particularly enjoyed humiliating the Guard Regiments stationed in St. Petersburg.

BELOW **Paul I appears as the perfect family man in this 1800 portrait. In fact, he alienated all around him including his son and heir, Alexander.**

Paul also issued a stream of decrees and rules that seemed designed to make his subjects' lives as miserable as possible. Just a selection from a long list includes: All nobles had to eat at one o'clock; a 10 p.m. curfew was imposed in the major cities; all things French were banned; everyone, including pregnant women, had to dismount from their carriages and kneel down in the muddy streets to greet the Czar if he happened to be passing; the waltz was prohibited, as were multicolored ribbons; children were not allowed outside unaccompanied by an adult lest they make too much noise; and sideburns were banned. To enforce these regulations, bands of armed dragoons roamed the streets of Russian cities. They attacked any passerby who was in breach.

ABOVE **Paul was the original "insufferable toad." He died by being choked with a scarf, beaten with a snuff box, and asphyxiated with a paper weight.**

Private printing presses were closed down. International trade was limited. Paul also alienated the nobles, by far the most powerful section of Russian society. Paul's predecessor, Czarina Catherine (1729–1796), had granted the nobles immunity from arrest, torture, and corporal punishment. The new Czar cancelled these protections. What's more, he interfered with the running of the great estates.

Like any good mad tyrant, Paul had a healthy dose of paranoia. He increased the powers of the "Secret Expedition of the Senate" (the Imperial security agency) and used arbitrary arrest and torture to clamp down on dissent. These punishments mainly fell on the upper classes and, while precise numbers are unknown, Alexander I (1777–1825) released around 12,000 political prisoners on his ascension to the throne. Friends and relatives of those arrested became suspects, and a feeling of fatalistic melancholia engulfed the elite of St. Petersburg.

Paul sought to ensure his safety. He felt insecure in the maze-like Winter Palace and built a brand-new residence in St. Petersburg, the Mikhailovsky Zamok. This had the latest security features, including a moat complete with drawbridges to prevent hostile attacks. Secret stairways leading under the moat and to safety were built into the palace, as were numerous boltholes should he need to flee. Five thousand workers labored on this monumental palace andPaul was so determined to move into it as

ABOVE **Paul I thought the state-of-the-art security features of St. Michael's Palace would save him. Soon after its completion he was dead.**

soon as possible that he had large iron plates put against the plaster-work to ensure it dried quickly. The whole enterprise cost many millions of roubles. Paul should have saved his money; he was assassinated three weeks after moving into his fine new residence.

Meanwhile, his delusional behavior and excessive outbursts of anger continued to escalate. For many in the military, the final straw was a harebrained plan to march an army through the Middle East and Afghanistan to invade British possessions in India. Two officers who felt they had been shabbily treated, Count Pahlen and General Levin Bennigsen, plotted to remove the Mad and Bad Czar.

Paul heard whispers of the plot and summoned long-time supporters from distant estates with the intention of increasing his security. Chief conspirator Pahlen intercepted one of these messages and decided the moment had come to get rid of the Czar. The Semyonovsky guards took over duty at the palace. Their commander was

THE EMPEROR TURNED PURPLE WITH ANGER WHEN HE SAW THAT SOMEONE HAD REPLACED THE NORMAL GUARD TROOPS WITH THE PREOBRAZHENSKY REGIMENT, WHOM PAUL SAW AS DANGEROUS JACOBINS.

sympathetic to the conspirators and had been humiliated by Paul once too often. Crucially, Pahlen gained the tacit support of Alexander. He assured the heir that Paul would not be harmed but would merely be forced to sign a letter of abdication. It was planned that General Bennigsen should take six conspirators to the Czar's bedroom at midnight and seize Paul before putting him under house arrest. Alexander was reassured by Pahlen that his father would be able to live a full life confined to his palace complex.

Pahlen enlisted the commander of the Semyonovsky guard and plied 60 of his officers with alcohol. They all knew of the plot and the night became more boisterous as the wine and vodka flowed. One conspirator asked what would happen if the Czar offered resistance. Pahlen replied: "Gentlemen, you cannot make an omelet without breaking eggs."

That night, Paul had 17 guests to dinner, including Alexander and General Kutuzov. Paul had been fretful and suspicious all day but relaxed a little when showing off his new porcelain dinner service. He noticed that Alexander had little appetite and suggested he should see the royal doctor, the Scottish physician James Wylie.

The officer of the guard brought the nightly security report. The emperor turned purple with anger when he saw that someone had replaced the normal guard troops with the Preobrazhensky Regiment, whom Paul saw as dangerous Jacobins (the left-wing extremists of the French Revolution). He retired to his chamber and locked the door with two valets stationed outside, dressed in full hussar rig and armed with sabers.

BELOW LEFT **Pyotr Alexeevich Palen earned no reward for his part in the conspiracy. He was exiled from Alexander's court soon after the assassination.**

BELOW RIGHT **Count Bennigsen was rewarded with many military commands by the new emperor Alexander. He fought many crucial battles against Napoleon.**

During the bitterly cold evening of March 11, 1801, the officer on duty let in 18 thoroughly intoxicated conspirators led by General Bennigsen. The two valets were overcome, the door broken down, and the bedroom entered. A single candle was burning, and it was at first impossible to make out where Paul was; but then he was discovered hiding behind a screen, shaking in terror. Bennigsen declared: "Sire, you have ceased to reign and we are arresting you on the orders of Czar Alexander." Paul, still inebriated himself, was unsure if it was a dream or reality. Then he began to argue, heaping streams of abuse on his guards.

The officers, even more drunk than their ruler, allowed their years of frustration at parade bashing and petty fault-finding to burst out and seized the Czar. Nicholas Zubov struck him across the left temple with a heavy snuff box. A sickening cracking noise filled the chamber, but this served only to spur on the attackers. Another seized a silk scarf and began to garrote the royal neck. Finally, one assassin held a malachite paperweight against Paul's windpipe and pressed down with all his weight until his victim stopped breathing. No one could be certain who actually accomplished the murder, but Paul was declared dead two minutes short of March 12, 1801. Pahlen told Alexander that his father had died of apoplexy. James Wylie, the court doctor, knew which side his bread was buttered on and agreed with this diagnosis, recording it as the official cause of death.

ABOVE **Alexander later attained fame by conquering Napoleon, but he never escaped the shame of being involved in regicide.**

LEFT **Paul I was set upon by his drunken guardsmen. The royal surgeon attributed the cause of death to an apoplectic fit.**

Alexander was devastated and became incapacitated with grief. It was only his wife who persuaded him to get a grip and assume the reins of power. Nevertheless, he remained haunted by his well-intentioned involvement in the plot for the rest of his days.

And Alexander did prove to be an inspired leader. It is unlikely that Paul I could have defeated Napoleon in 1812 and carried the war to Paris in 1814.

The Deadly Snowball

Alexander II (1818–1881), Emperor of Russia, survived more assassination attempts than Adolf Hitler. Ascending the throne on March 2, 1855, he immediately began a program of reform. This included the historic emancipation of the serfs in 1861, setting up local councils, abolishing capital punishment, regulating the judicial system, and encouraging the development of railway lines and industrialization. He had little interest in war and signed several treaties seeking to guarantee peace in Europe.

All of these positive actions should have earned him the gratitude of a loyal population. Instead, it earned him the implacable hatred of a small group of revolutionaries whose constant attacks on the Czar's person led to his emotional breakdown.

The first attempt was in 1866 when a young revolutionary student, Dmitry Karakozov, arrived in St. Petersburg with the aim of killing his Czar. On April 4, he went to the gates of the Summer Palace and, seeing his intended victim, pulled out his gun and took aim, but an apprentice hatmaker, Osip Komissarov, jostled the would-be assassin, causing his shots to miss. Karakozov tried to flee but was arrested and later publicly hanged. Komissarov was elevated to the nobility and awarded a fat pension.

BELOW **Dmitry Karakozov's attempt to assassinate Tsar Alexander II in St. Petersburg on April 4, 1866, was the first of many.**

ABOVE **At the 1867 World Fair, Alexander and his two sons narrowly escaped bullets fired by a Polish patriot protesting against the subjugation of his homeland.**

Another solo effort was made by a Polish immigrant during the 1867 World's Fair. The Czar was travelling in a carriage with his two sons and Napoleon III. The would-be killer's modified double-barreled pistol misfired, and the only individual to take a bullet was a nearby horse.

Alexander was able to treat these as the random attacks of a few madmen. However, in 1879 things got a lot more serious. A teacher, Alexander Soloviev, walked toward the Czar with a pistol in his hand. Soloviev did not try to hide his intentions, and Alexander easily evaded five bullets by zigzagging as he bolted away. Soloviev couldn't evade the noose and died soon after.

Some of Alexander's key supporters were also targets of assassins during this period. The head of the St. Petersburg police was stabbed outside his office, and one of the key enforcers, Prince Dmitri Kropotkin, was killed. These random attacks on government officials were replaced by more sustained attempts by revolutionary groups such as Narodnaya Volya, "The Will of the People." Like most fanatics, this hardcore band of assassins purported to represent the majority of the population, whereas they were really just a small group of largely unhinged murderers. This organization viewed itself as an alternative government and in August 1879 formally condemned "Alexander Romanov" to death.

Alexander took steps to crack down on these revolutionary groups. The measures employed reversed some of the earlier positive reforms. Three special governor generals were given the responsibility for clearing opposition. They embarked on a series of raids, searches, arrests, expulsions, imprisonments, and executions. They had full judicial authority to arrest, sentence, and execute. The condemned had no right of appeal, the sale of firearms was prohibited, and subversive publications could be closed down. While hundreds of reactionaries were arrested, others saw this as more evidence of why the Czar had to be killed.

Despite all the measures taken, the Narodnaya Volya were particularly adept at avoiding the police and emerged as a real threat to the Czar. Their first attempt was carried out when they blew up the royal train. Alexander was becoming more security conscious, and whenever he traveled by rail he was preceded by a locomotive with several carriages, used to test the safety of the rails and carry the royal luggage. He usually followed in a second train. However, on November 19, 1879, a fault with the luggage locomotive led to the Czar and his family traveling on the first train. The revolutionaries blew up the second train, leading to several people being injured and three carriages leaving the rails. While escaping physically unscathed, Alexander was deeply traumatized. "Am I such a wild beast that they should hound me to death?"

BELOW **Despite an outward show of calm, Alexander II of Russia became increasingly despondent due to the repeated assassination attempts.**

Further protective measures were taken. Bulletproof wadding was sewn into Alexander's uniforms, and the royal carriages were lined with bulletproof steel. Alexander was escorted by a veritable phalanx of security whenever he ventured beyond the palace walls, and his itineraries were kept secret until the last moment. The Czar was advised to stop smoking lest a bomb be planted in his favorite cigars!

All to no avail. A massive bomb was detonated right in the heart of the Winter Palace. A trained carpenter called Stephen Khalturin managed to obtain a job doing repairs in the basement. He was a member of the Narodnaya Volya, and the fact that he was allowed to get work in such a place surely shows the incompetence of the Imperial security. Every day he carried in a few sticks of dynamite and gradually assembled a huge charge just below the dining room.

Once again, Alexander escaped by the skin of his teeth. A dinner party was planned for 6 p.m. on February 5, 1880. One of the attendees was half an hour late, and the dinner guests were being marshalled by the Czar to enter the dining room when the bomb went off. The whole palace was shaken to its core, and the dining room was all but vaporized. Ten members of the Finnish Guard Regiment were killed outright and 45 wounded.

The Czar escaped physical injury, but the morale of the royal family was shattered. He seemed to age 20 years, and this was made worse by threatening letters in black envelopes left around the palace, delivered by some subversive servant. Each letter stated he would not live beyond February 18.

The campaign of terror also affected the inhabitants of St. Petersburg. Members of Narodnaya Volya dug tunnels under roads and installed bombs in case the Czar should pass. They didn't mind if they were discovered, as it escalated pressure on the police and advertised their cause. Patrons would not attend the opera if they heard the royal family was attending, and many wealthy citizens left town. Curfews were imposed, and the Czar stayed virtually a prisoner in his palaces.

However, he did stick to one routine, and this was to be his downfall. On Sundays, he usually inspected the guards at Mikhailovsky Zamok before visiting his cousin. Narodnaya Volya decided to mine one of the streets leading to the palace using a shop as their cover. The attempt was organized by Sophia Perovskaya, who took the precaution of arming four terrorists with bombs and arranging them on an alternative route.

On the fateful day, March 13, 1881, the Czar was advised by his chief security officer to cancel his visit to the Mikhailovsky Zamok due to alarming intelligence reports. Alexander said he had so much protection with his Cossack outriders and bodyguards that if he was still not safe, he may as well abdicate. On the morning, he seemed particularly happy and carefree, as if 20 years had dropped from his frame.

BELOW **Another fine day in St. Petersburg. On March 13, 1881, left-wing assassins finally got their man.**

ABOVE **Alexander should have fled when the first bomb was thrown at his carriage. Instead, he stayed to help, and a second bomb inflicted a mortal wound.**

But as he was returning to the palace, Perovskaya'a assassins struck. Nikolai Rysakov threw the first bomb. It damaged the Czar's carriage and killed two Cossacks. Although he was urged to flee the scene, Alexander tried to help the wounded. A policeman thanked God that the Czar was unhurt, but at that moment Ignatius Grinevitsky ran at the Czar and threw a nitroglycerine bomb disguised as a snowball at his feet.

The resulting explosion shook windows hundreds of yards (meters) away. The Czar's face was streaming with blood, and one eye had popped out with the force of the explosion. Both of his legs were severed below the knee, and only the intense cold stopped him bleeding out on the spot. The assassin and 20 others in the crowd were also killed. Although the Czar was immediately taken to the palace, any measures, such as rubbing his temples with ether, proved fruitless, and the sovereign died within an hour. The future Nicholas II (see page 61) was present at the death of his grandfather, and no doubt he was shaken to the core.

Alexander III (1845–1894) was installed on the throne. The conspirators were arrested and hanged. Any liberal reforms were cancelled, and the new Czar ruled his empire with an iron fist of repression and violence.

The Shot That Sparked a War

It is not often that a person can reach out and almost touch the most world-shattering event in modern history—but you can in the Museum of Military History in Vienna. Perched on a hill overlooking the Ringstrasse that encircles the old town is the former arsenal. This has been converted into the Heeresgeschichtliches Museum (HGM) and in pride of place is the military uniform of Archduke Franz Ferdinand. Separating this historical artifact is only a thin pane of glass, allowing the viewer to get within 1 inch of the assassinated Archduke's uniform. If you look very carefully, you can see a tiny hole just where the collar meets the front of the tunic. This insignificant hole traces the path of one bullet that changed European history in the 20th century and brought about more than 70 million deaths. More obvious is the dried and encrusted blood, for that small bullet led to the archduke bleeding copiously down the front of his uniform and on to his trousers. The stain is still there, although now it has turned white.

Archduke Franz Ferdinand (b. 1863) was gunned down on June 28, 1914 in Sarajevo by Gavrilo Princip, a young recruit to the "Black Hand" terrorist organization. In Serbian, it was called "Ujedinjenje ili Smrt" (Union or Death). Princip was a rank amateur, barely able to aim and too inexperienced to count his shots. One other attempt had been made earlier in the day when an associate of Princip had lobbed a bomb at the Imperial cavalcade. How was it that a group of poorly trained amateurs had been able to take out the heir to the Austro-Hungarian throne?

BELOW **Archduke Franz Ferdinand married Sophie against the Emperor's wishes. This may have indirectly led to his death.**

Blame must be laid at the foot of General Oskar Potiorek and his Imperial master, Emperor Franz Joseph I (1830–1916). Franz Ferdinand had clashed with the emperor, his uncle, on many occasions. Franz had fallen madly in love with the Czech countess Sophie Chotek and married her in 1900. Franz Joseph I disapproved of the marriage and tried to dissuade his nephew from the "unsuitable" match, but to no avail: a rift was opened between the emperor and his heir.

During the years leading up to 1914, the two had found another cause of dissension. In 1908, the Austrians had annexed the largely Slavic province of Bosnia-Herzegovina. The fiercely proud and independent Slavic state of Serbia wanted the Austrians out. The archduke wanted to reconcile the different groups and negotiate a peaceful resolution. His uncle wanted no such thing. The Hapsburgs had spent the last 700 years bashing up other countries and adding them to their empire, and Emperor Franz Joseph wanted to continue the tradition. He wanted an excuse to hammer the Serbs and conquer their country. It's likely, therefore, that Franz Joseph I wanted his heir to be killed. Potiorek made so many blunders that either he was incredibly stupid or he was acting on orders from on high to facilitate the killing of the heir.

Princip was a 19-year-old student born on July 13, 1894, in the Bosnian village of Obljaj. He was the second son of a poor peasant, and he grew up to be an earnest, bookish child, usually alone and not mingling with other boys his age. He was fortunate that his elder brother had founded a successful lumber business and was able to pay for Princip's education. He was enrolled at the Merchants' School, downtown Sarajevo. The term "still waters run deep" would be an apt description of the young man; he soon became obsessed with revolutionary literature and spent so much time agitating in anti-Austrian demonstrations that he was expelled. He walked the 186-mile (300-kilometer) journey to Belgrade, where he joined other Pan-Slavs (those who believed in uniting Russian and Serbian Slavs in a Pan-Slavic empire). This network spent its days frequenting coffee houses and discussing Marxist ideology, among other topics.

BELOW **Franz Joseph I was determined to sort out "the Serbian question." The assassination of Franz Ferdinand gave him the perfect excuse to attack.**

At the end of March 1914, it was announced that the Hapsburg heir apparent was going to visit Sarajevo to inspect army manoeuvers. Princip was shown a newspaper clipping with this news and, catching up with some friends on a park bench, he casually suggested that it would be a perfect time to assassinate Franz Ferdinand. A small cabal formed and began to discuss how best to carry out this assassination. Weapons were needed, and through their underground network the young men were introduced to Colonel Dimitrijevic (code name: Apis). He was a ruthless operator and had been planning for several years to kill the archduke. He saw Franz Ferdinand as a real threat due to his moderate views. The future emperor was in favor of liberal reforms and was planning to give Serbians a greater degree of independence within the empire. He even considered making them semi-autonomous with full voting rights. These reforms would have turned many Serbs against radical violent methods and defused any potentially violent mass protests or rebellions. Like most assassins, the thing that Apis feared most was a peaceful outcome.

Weapons were sourced for the four conspirators. Each was provided with a Belgian-made 9mm automatic pistol; each slug could stop a bull and the rapid-fire feature was perfect for close-in work in a crowded situation. The four were also given six Serb military bombs with a 12-second time-delay fuse. The assassins all agreed to commit suicide if caught and were issued with papers filled with cyanide potassium.

Before the attack, Sophie had a premonition that they should not travel into the heart of Serbian nationalism and pleaded with her husband to cancel the visit. It was planned for June 28, the feast of St Vitus, the most sacred day in the Serbian calendar. But Ferdinand was made of stern stuff and refused to cancel. The two arrived at the Bosnian capital at separate times but were reunited after Franz had observed military manoeuvers on June 26 and 27.

ABOVE **Dragutin Dimitrijević, code name Apis, was the mastermind behind the Black Hand's attack on the Archduke.**

Security arrangements were botched from the moment the royal couple arrived on the morning of June 28. General Potiorek met them at Sarajevo railway station with a total of three local policemen as the only security detail. He apologized for the lack of personnel and said more were coming soon. Due to another oversight, the security detail that had been shadowing the archduke for the past weeks was left behind when the royal couple were driven into town. The agents jumped into several open-topped tourers and proceeded into the center of Sarajevo.

It was here that the first attack was made. The main road into the heart of town was festooned with banners, bunting, and bouquets. Potiorek obviously had no compunction about advertising the route of the targeted couple. And all along the route, Princip and his co-conspirators waited; armed with pistols and bombs, they were ready to stalk and execute their prey. The chief of Sarajevo police was aware of the danger. Several times he had complained to the governor, saying that he only had 120 gendarmes to guard the entire route, which was several miles long. Potiorek chose to ignore the police chief's concerns.

The first attempt was made by Nedeljko Cabrinovic, who hefted one of the bombs at the archduke's car. As the square bomb spun toward the archduke, trailing smoke from its burning fuse, Franz proved he was no coward. He stood to swat the bomb away and it bounced on the retracted roof at the rear of the vehicle and on to the road, where it exploded under the second car. Several onlookers, as well as some of the security detail in the second car, were wounded. It is here that Franz Ferdinand perhaps proved himself to be more brave than clever. He demanded that his vehicle

RIGHT The assassination of the Archduke and his wife the Duchess in Sarajevo, from the illustrated supplement of *Le Petit Journal.*

stop to allow the party to inspect the damage. Shrapnel had hit the royal car and a splinter had grazed his beloved wife's neck.

Cabrinovic proved what an amateur he was. He had completely forgotten about the 12-second fuse and thown the bomb too early.

The cavalcade proceeded to the town hall, where a furious Franz Ferdinand could barely contain his anger. Many of the attending officials argued that the royal couple should wait for military units to be brought into town to protect them. Ferdinand vetoed these suggestions and said he desired to go to the hospital to visit his wounded officers. He asked Potiorek if there was a chance another attempt would be made. The governor declared it extremely unlikely and said he would accept full responsibility for the couple's safety.

As a result, arrangements were changed, and rather than splitting up and attending different events, the royal couple would stay together and visit the museum, followed by a visit to Sarajevo hospital. However, Potiorek didn't tell his own personal chauffeur, driving the royal car, of the change of plans. As the convoy moved from Sarajevo town hall along Appel Quay, two cars preceding Franz Ferdinand made a turn toward the museum. Not able to brake and turn in time, the royal driver braked sharply and came to a halt. Princip couldn't believe his luck. Steeling himself for the violent act, he stepped forward and delivered his two lead missiles into the royal couple. Standing less than 5 feet (1.5 meters) from the car, he barely took aim and even turned his head away when firing the second bullet.

The first bullet hit Franz Ferdinand in the neck before piercing his jugular, making him bleed out in a matter of minutes. His last words were to his beloved wife: "Sophie, look after the children." But she was in no shape to do her husband's bidding: Princip's second bullet had struck her abdomen. Potiorek ordered his chauffeur to drive to his residence. Sophie was dead on arrival and Franz Ferdinand finally gave up the ghost on a sofa in the residence. (The sofa is still on display below the uniform at the museum, along with the car, complete with shrapnel holes.)

Princip's statement shows how easily this untrained assassin managed to kill his targets:

> *"When the second car arrived, I recognized the heir to the throne. But as I saw a lady sitting next to him I reflected for a moment whether I should shoot or not. At the same moment I was filled with a peculiar feeling and I aimed at Franz Ferdinand from the pavement—which was made easier because the car was proceeding slower at the moment. Where I aimed I do not know. But I know I aimed in the direction of the heir apparent. I believed that I fired twice, perhaps more, because I was so excited. Whether I hit the victims or not, I cannot tell, because instantly people started hitting me."*

After shooting the royal couple, Princip tried to turn the pistol on himself, but he was seized by an onlooker. His bomb fell out of his pocket and although he was being viciously beaten by security and onlookers he tried to swallow his cyanide, but this too failed. Most of his co-conspirators were executed, but being too young for the death penalty, Princip died a lonely death in a cell in Kleine Festung (the "small fort") outside Prague.

Anti-Serb riots erupted throughout Bosnia, and Potiorek finally ordered the army into town to restore order. Emperor Franz Joseph had the excuse he wanted. A catalogue of demands was delivered to the Serbian government in Belgrade. They agreed to all but one. Even Kaiser Wilhelm II of Germany stated that the Serbians had been reasonable so that there was no need for an attack by Austria. The Austrians would not be budged, however, and opened fire on Belgrade on July 28, exactly one month after the assassination. Russia mobilized to protect her Serbian ally. France, Germany, and Great Britain all followed suit, and World War I commenced.

BELOW **A stunned crowd considers the possible repercussions of the attack on the heir to the Austro-Hungarian throne.**

Caught on Camera

On October 9, 1934, history was made. It was the first time the assassination of a king was caught on motion picture. King Alexander I of Yugoslavia was in France to stitch up an alliance with the French to counter the resurgent Nazi German state. As Alexander and the French foreign minister drove through central Marseille, there was a cameraman there to film the festivities. Suddenly, right in front of the cameraman, an assassin jumped out and fired into the vehicle. The footage shows the confusion as the Bulgarian attacker, Vlado Chernozemski, is almost beaten to death. Poignantly, the last shot shows the king, slumped in the back of the car as his life ebbs.

A Royal Massacre

The Czar and his family were not so much assassinated as exterminated. On July 17, 1918, Nicholas II, the Czarina Alexandra, the Czarevitch (heir) Alexei, and their four daughters Olga, Tatiana, Maria, and Anastasia were all taken to the basement of the Ipatiev House in Yekaterinburg. Here they would die in a shower of blood and gore.

Czar Nicholas had been deposed in the first of two Russian revolutions in 1917. He abdicated on March 15, less than four years after celebrating the tercentennial of the Romanov dynasty. When war broke out between forces largely loyal to the Czar (the White Army) and the Bolsheviks (the Red Army), the Romanov family was removed by the Bolsheviks to a relative backwater—the town of Yekaterinburg in the Ural Mountains. Lenin saw the Czar as a potential rallying point for White Russians and, as such, a threat to his revolution.

There are many theories as to who ordered the killing of Nicholas Romanov's family, and various reasons for the decision. Yekaterinburg was something of a frontier town on the eastern edge of European Russia. Established to exploit the rich mineral resources in the area, it was surrounded by forests and occupied a strategic point in the Ural Basin. By late June 1918, it was obvious that the town would fall either to approaching royalist forces or to the Czech Legion. At night, the rumble of gunfire and the flash of artillery shells could be seen on the horizon. Within the hotels in the center of town, royalist sympathizers had been noticed by the local Cheka, and it seems some communication had been established with the captive

ABOVE Tsar Nicholas II and family in happier times (1913). From left to right: Olga, Maria, Nikolay, Alexandra, Anastasia, Alexey, and Tatiana.

Romanovs. To test the waters, the Cheka sent notes contained in hampers of food, pretending to set up a rescue attempt. Nicholas and his family maintained the correspondence and packed, ready for their liberation. This, of course, never materialized, but the Yekaterinburg Soviet (Workers' and Soldiers' Council) now knew what the royals would do should a rescue be launched.

On July 4, the easy-going guards who were in charge of the royal family were relieved of their duty, and the much less congenial Yakov Yurovsky, a hard-nosed Bolshevik, became their jailer. There were concerns that the previous personnel had become too close to the Romanovs, and one young man may even have carried out an illicit affair with one of the royal daughters. The new guards were Chekists to a man.

An air of despondency settled over the captives. The young prince's health was rapidly failing, and even the formerly bright young duchesses seemed depressed. The windows of the Ipatiev House had previously been painted over, and long strolls in the garden, which Nicholas had particularly enjoyed, were stopped. Sitting in their gloomy surrounds, the royal family were perhaps becoming resigned to their fate.

On July 12, it was announced to the Ural Soviet that Lenin in Moscow would let the local Bolsheviks decide the fate of the Czar and his family. On the following day, Yurovsky was given the order to execute them. Plans for the massacre went forward swiftly. Members of the Ural Soviet searched for an appropriate place to dump the bodies, and an abandoned mine shaft, 12 miles (20 kilometers) from Yekaterinburg, was found. It was named the "four brothers" mine after some large trees that surrounded the site. An old flatbed Fiat truck was requisitioned to transport the corpses.

On the night of July 16, Yurovsky swung into action. He had sourced a range of weapons and allowed his executioners to choose their own gun. On his desk were up to 15 pistols; Mausers, Colts, Brownings, Nagants, and even a Smith and Wesson. Most of the 11 killers took two guns. Yurovsky chose a Mauser and a Colt. The drunken Ermakov, a notorious Cheka executioner, already had two Russian Nagants strapped to his belt, but he was handed another Nagant and a Mauser. The assassination squad were told of the plan and each was given a target to dispatch once the shooting began. They took station in a room in the basement of the Ipatiev House, waiting until they were summoned.

Meanwhile, the Romanovs were roused from their slumber. Told that an evacuation was imminent, they were instructed to pack all their belongings. The family was not rushed; Yurovsky did not want any panic. Forty-five minutes later, the family was shepherded into a small room in the basement. The royals and their retainers seemed relieved; finally, they were getting out of the stuffy Siberian prison.

Playing his part to the end, Yurovsky asked them to wait in the room while the truck was fetched. He ordered that three chairs be brought into the room, one each for Alexei and his parents. The three sat in a row near the middle of the room while the young duchesses leaned

BELOW **By April 1917 the Tsar and his family were held by the Provisional Government. Soon the Bolsheviks would seize them.**

against the wall behind them. A dim light bulb swung gently in the grim room, reducing them all to hazy silhouettes.

The Fiat was moved nearer to the house, and the driver began gunning the engine.

Once his preparations were complete, Yurovsky collected his squad and led them into the corridor beyond the closed double doors shielding the Romanovs. At 2:15 a.m. he opened the doors and stepped into the room. The executioners followed, crowding around their leader, four in the front rank and five behind them.

Yurovsky ordered the family to stand. He pulled from his pocket a piece of paper. Barely able to read it in the dim light, he announced: "In view of the fact that your relatives continue their offensive against Soviet Russia, the Presidium of the Ural Regional Soviet has decided to sentence you to death." Nicholas stood aghast and asked to hear the order again. One of the duchesses cried "Oh, my God! No!" Nicholas looked at Yurovsky. Frozen in shock, he cried "What? What?"

"This," Yurovsky answered, pulling out his pistol. Aiming it at the Czar's chest, he fired the first bullet of the fusillade that was to follow. The royal chest exploded in a bloody mess as the other members of the squad pulled out their pistols and started firing. In the heat of the moment, they forgot their assigned targets, and most of the first volley crashed into the Czar. The bullets ripped through Nicholas's lungs and heart, and he toppled forward to the floor.

So closely packed were the executioners, with the back row discharging their firearms right next to the heads of the four in the front row, that the front rank had powder burns on their necks. The reports were deafening in the small room and even visibility shrank to almost nothing as the room filled with smoke. Only the legs of the victims could be seen as they staggered back and forth or tried to shelter in the corner.

The smoke cleared momentarily to reveal the duchesses huddled together. The Czarina still stood erect in the center of the room. The drunken Ermakov raised his Mauser and fired just as she turned away. The bullet slammed into her left temple and exited on

BELOW **Yakov Yurovsky was a hardened Chekist who believed in class war. He assumed responsibility for the custody of the Romanovs before organizing their execution.**

ABOVE **Ipatiev House. To the left of this picture is the basement where the Romanovs were gunned down by Yurovsky and his crew.**

the right side, spraying blood and brain tissue all over her four daughters. The Empress fell to the floor and moved no longer.

Plaster dust, ricochets, and smoke made the room toxic and now reduced visibility to naught. The double doors were thrown open in an attempt to clear the air. Many of the execution squad staggered out into the corridor to vomit and clear tears from their stinging eyes. Low moans and screams still emanated from the deathly basement.

After several minutes, the cohort of assassins once again crossed the threshold to finish their ghastly job. The family doctor was still alive, trying to get up on one elbow. A shot from a Mauser finished him off and slammed him into the floor in a shower of gore.

The Czarevitch was still sitting in his chair, untouched by any bullet, drenched in his father's blood, wide-eyed and rigid with terror. Two assassins emptied their clip into his chest and he slid to the floor. He was still breathing, and it seemed Ermakov was the only man who could finish the job. He pulled an 8-inch (20-centimeter) triangular bayonet out of its scabbard and stabbed the boy repeatedly. Unknown to the assassin, the boy had secreted jewels and precious metals in pouches next to his chest. This gave him some measure of protection, and it fell to Yurovsky to pull the Colt from his belt, step over the other bloodied bodies, and fire two shots into the Romanov heir's head.

Huddled in the corner, spectators to the carnage, were Olga, Tatiana, and Anastasia. They cowered with their arms protecting each other. Yurovsky and Ermakov reloaded and approached the screaming girls. With the two killers almost upon them, the girls tried to rise and flee. Too late. Yurovsky fired a heavy-caliber bullet into the back of

Tatiana's head. It ripped open her skull and blew the right side of her face over Olga. He kicked Olga to the floor and shot her in the head.

Maria and Anastasia then received the full attention of the assassins. Ermakov again tried to use the bayonet, but both girls had a bodice filled with jewels, and the bayonet would not pierce these inadvertent protections. They too had to be shot. Ermakov entered into a blood frenzy and leapt around the room stabbing the now dead bodies with his bayonet. He jumped on the Czar with such violence that the point of the bayonet cracked Nicholas's sternum and pinned his corpse to the floor.

The royal family was dead.

What was planned as an efficient execution had turned into a horrific gore fest, particularly for the four duchesses who had

BELOW This reconstruction of the assassination of the Romanovs conveys some of the chaos of the massacre. In reality gun smoke reduced visibility dramatically.

remained alive to witness it for at least ten minutes before they were killed in the most terrible manner imaginable. The small room was covered with a "liver-like" torrent of blood. This did not dismay the execution squad as they moved among the corpses, stripping them of jewels and treasure. They also found pillows filled with booty in the luggage and ripped them open, covering the entire mess in feathers.

The bodies were pulled out of the charnel house, loaded on to the Fiat, and taken to their burial place. Once again, Yurovsky made a frightful hash of his job. The original mine shaft proved too shallow to conceal the bodies, and they persisted in floating up through a thick layer of liquid scum, coming to rest in an unsightly mass of pale corpse skin. It was decided to find another site, and while transporting the bodies, the Fiat was bogged several times before breaking down. Attempts were made to burn the Czarevitch, and gallons of petrol were poured on his frail corpse. Most of the petrol ran into the soil, and the young prince's remains were only charred.

When a body is subjected to fire, whether doused with gasoline or some other fuel, the process is the same. First the epidermal (skin) layer chars, along with subcutaneous tissues and fat. This has the effect of searing the body as if it were a steak on a hot griddle. A kind of protective shell is thus created around the rest of the body, preserving organs, tissues, and bone while keeping moisture within the corpse. Internal organs may be seared or boiled but they are still largely intact. The open-air crematorium employed by the Bolsheviks ensured there was no concentrated heat to do the job properly. Despairing of ever disposing of the corpses, Yurovsky finally had a pit enlarged and the family tossed in. Acid was poured over the bodies before the pit was filled in and railway sleepers laid atop the grim graves.

The Bolsheviks still weren't finished in their determination to destroy the Romanov family and bring in a new classless utopia. The Ural Soviet ordered the execution of the remaining royal entourage. Countess Anastasia Hendrikova, Mademoiselle Catherine Schneider, and Alexei Volkov had been attendants in the royal household. They were marched into a small field before being shot in the back.

In January 1919, the four last grand dukes of the Romanov dynasty were pulled out of their cells in a St. Petersburg prison and executed before being buried in a mass grave along with other victims of the Red Terror.

Finally, an expedition in 1991 retrieved remains from Pig's Meadow, where Nicholas and his family were buried. DNA testing proved that the remains were those of the last Czar and Czarina of the Romanovs and three of their precious daughters (their other two children, Maria and Alexei, were unearthed in 2007). They were given a state funeral and reburied in St. Petersburg cathedral on July 17, 1998, the 80th anniversary of their death; and in 2000 they were canonized by the Russian Orthodox Church, something they would surely have appreciated.

Political Leaders

Just as many kings and emperors were killed by political rivals, some modern political leaders have been assassinated, even though they have gained power through democratic elections. Many of the political leaders in this chapter had the precious gift of charisma and were so popular with their supporters that they were unlikely to be voted out of office. Some created profound change in their country and were admired around the world. This success led to their downfall. If political opponents could not remove these leaders through the ballot box, they would remove them with a bullet or a bomb.

Giuliano de' Medici

At the height of the Italian Renaissance, Giuliano de' Medici (1453–1478) was murdered. Assassination was a common occurrence on the Italian peninsula, which was divided into myriad city states, feudal holdings, and ecclesiastical possessions. Some of the most powerful of these states were of course Milan, Venice, Genoa, Rome, and Florence. Within each domain, different factions jostled for power using poison, crossbows, swords, and daggers to remove opponents.

The killing of Giuliano on April 26, 1478 was remarkable for several reasons: it occurred during one of the most holy events in the Christian calendar, it was sponsored by Pope Sixtus IV, and it was carried out by a Catholic priest.

For several decades, the Tuscan city of Florence had risen to great wealth and influence under the rule of the Medici family. Piero de' Medici (1416–1469) had sired two sons, Lorenzo (1449–1492) and Giuliano. These two became the rulers of Florence after the death of their father, and both were exceedingly popular. It seemed the Medici had a never-ending monopoly of power on the great city. Rivals were determined to mount a coup and take over.

Chief among these was Pope Sixtus IV. He saw Florence as a military and commercial threat to his Roman Papal states and coveted the great wealth of the city state. He aligned himself with, among others, the Pazzi. This family was one of the great old Florentine families, who had seen their wealth and prestige gradually ebb away with the advent of the Medici. They were determined to win it back, and on the eve of Easter Sunday 1478 mercenaries and armed retainers of the Pazzi, with funding from the Holy See, gathered in Florence to prepare for the coup.

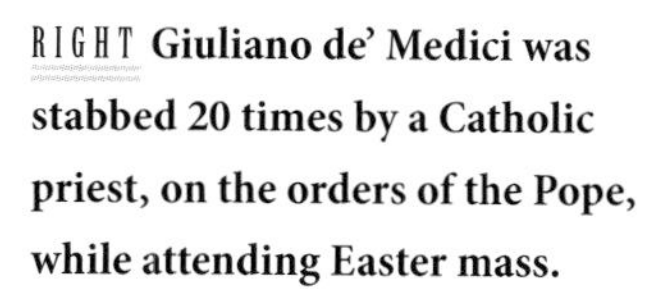

RIGHT **Giuliano de' Medici was stabbed 20 times by a Catholic priest, on the orders of the Pope, while attending Easter mass.**

The high mass of Easter Sunday was one religious event that no self-respecting Florentine could miss. The wealthiest Florentines gathered in the Duomo in the heart of the walled city. Toward the front of the congregation, Lorenzo and his younger brother Giuliano sat side by side. Behind them sat two assassins. One was an anointed priest called Francesco de' Pazzi. He was armed with a long dagger, and he knew that in Pazzi residences throughout the city there was a small army waiting to seize control.

At the height of the ceremony as the Cardinal raised the Sacred Host high in the air and as the congregation bowed their heads in this most holy of moments, Francesco and his compatriot struck. He pulled a dagger from his princely robes and leapt upon the younger brother. Giuliano was taken completely by surprise and was stabbed in the back more than twenty times. He lay mortally wounded on the cathedral floor. Lorenzo was more fortunate. Despite a bad neck wound, he was surrounded by armed retainers and hurried from the scene.

Fighting erupted in the Duomo and throughout the streets of Florence as the two factions fought for supremacy. Sixtus's man in Florence, Archbishop Salviati of Pisa, tried to form a new government, but when it became known that Lorenzo survived, the Florentine population turned on the conspirators and took a bloody revenge. Salviati was hung from a palace window next to Francesco Pazzi. Two hundred members of this family were tortured, killed, mutilated, and tossed into the Arno.

Lorenzo went on to consolidate his rule and was soon known as Lorenzo the Great. The Pazzi were never a threat again, and the Pope earned a reputation as a ruthless schemer.

LEFT **The tomb of Giuliano de' Medici in the Medici Chapel, Florence, is widely held to be one of Michelangelo's most stunning achievements.**

ABOVE On April 9, 1865, General Lee surrendered to General Grant. Five days later, Grant was scheduled to go to the theater with President Lincoln.

Death at the Theater

On April 9, 1865, at Appomattox Courthouse, General Robert E. Lee, leader of the Confederate Army, surrendered to his nemesis, General Ulysses S. Grant. Known throughout the North as "Unconditional Surrender Grant," the victor was conciliatory toward Lee. His terms were fair: All Confederate soldiers would be released and could return home under parole as long as they did not take up arms against the Union. All weapons and equipment were to be turned over to Union forces, although officers could keep their sidearms, swords, baggage, and horses.

This generosity of spirit echoed President Lincoln's own attitude to the defeated rebels. He believed that as long as the defeated states promised to cease further hostile activity, their property should be remitted, and any individual who showed repentance should be pardoned. This was in stark contrast to Lincoln's vice president, Andrew Johnson, who wanted to see the arrest, trial, and execution of all past rebel leaders. This promising hope of reconciliation between the estranged states was cut brutally short with one bullet fired into the back of the president's head, five days after the surrender at Appomattox.

ABOVE **The assassination of President Lincoln at Ford's Theater, Washington. John Wilkes Booth made a dramatic escape by sliding down a stage curtain.**

Twenty minutes after the curtain rose at Ford's Theatre in the fashionable center of Washington, DC, President Abraham Lincoln and his wife, Mary, entered the theatre. Although the performance was in the middle of the first act, it was stopped, and the band struck up "Hail to the Chief." The audience applauded but their welcome was somewhat muted as they expected to see a triumphant General Grant in the presidential party. Grant had been called away on urgent business.

Entering the box, the presidential couple sat toward the rear while their guests sat at the front. Lincoln had a roomy rocker, provided especially for him by the management. Bunting and curtains hid the president from the rest of the audience, although some stole a glance to see if Grant had arrived.

But minutes after the play resumed, all eyes were suddenly drawn to the box, attracted by a muffled explosion followed by smoke boiling out into the theatre. Out of the smoke emerged an individual holding a Derringer pistol in one hand and a dagger in the other. It was John Wilkes Booth, a failed actor and Southern sympathizer. He stood on the balustrade and, making the most of his time in the spotlight, leapt for the stage. Like most things he tried in life, this too was a failure, and his right spur caught on the red, white, and blue bunting, twisting him around so he broke his leg as he fell to the stage. His great theatrical moment was ruined. The assassin had intended to enthrall the audience with the Latin epithet "Sic semper tyrannis"—"Thus always to tyrants" (the state motto of Virginia). But all that came out was a muted curse that most could not hear. The actor then disappeared, stage left.

The delivery of Booth's speech may have gone awry, but his aim was true. Familiar with the layout of Ford's Theatre, he had found that the lock on the president's box was broken. Fortifying himself with a couple of brandies, he had pulled out his pistol and dagger and made his way to the box. Lincoln's guard had become bored and wandered off for a drink. Entering the box with the pistol in his left hand, he had placed it almost against the president's head and pulled the trigger. The ball entered the skull, tore through Lincoln's brain at an angle, and lodged behind his right eye. Pieces of the skull were found in the track of the bullet.

After a moment of stunned silence, calls went out for help. The first doctor on the scene thought that Lincoln was already dead. The president appeared to be asleep, with his knees relaxed and his head forward so that his chin rested on his chest. Checking for vital signs, the doctor found a faint pulse and lay Lincoln on the floor. The doctor was Charles A. Leale, and he had learned his trade on the battlefield. Familiar with the damage inflicted by musket balls, he knew that Lincoln's wound was mortal.

With the assistance of several soldiers, the wounded man was taken feet first down the stairs and into the street, an officer waving his sword to clear a path through the stunned onlookers. The president was taken to a dingy house just across the way and placed on a narrow cot owned by the Swedish tailor who lived there. Lincoln was too long for the bed, and his feet stuck comically out of the side.

It took eight hours for the bullet to finish its work. Initially, Lincoln appeared at rest, with rasping breath, a slow pulse, and hands and feet corpse-cold. The pupil of his left eye was much contracted while the right, with the bullet lodged behind the eye, was dilated. His face appeared peaceful, but his pupils did not respond to light.

LEFT **John Wilkes Booth was an actor with a flair for the dramatic. His last exit from the stage was marred when he broke his leg falling from Lincoln's box.**

BELOW **The Deadly Derringer wielded by Booth. One ball smashed into Lincoln's head, causing a mortal wound.**

Then his condition began to deteriorate. The left side of his face started to twitch violently, transforming the long features into a sneering rictus. On the right side, bloody bruising seemed to trail under the skin, and the eye filled with blood, bulging from its socket and seemingly ready to burst. Mary Lincoln screamed and had to be removed from the room. Secretary of State Stanton began dictating the letter announcing the death of the president. He heard a sob behind him where, unbeknown to him, Mary had heard the whole thing. She broke down, wailing, and could not be made to understand that her devoted husband was not yet dead.

As dawn approached, the waiting crowd beyond the tailor's parlor could hear from Lincoln's interrupted breathing, punctuated with loud groans, that he was approaching death. Then his breathing became fast and shallow, his chest heaving upward, and his lips turned blue.

At 7:22 on April 15, all signs of life ceased. The president was dead. "Now he belongs to the ages," intoned Stanton, as silver dollars were placed on Lincoln's closed eyes.

On April 26, Booth was hunted down by army regulars in a Virginia tobacco -drying barn. They set fire to it, and as he was flushed out they shot him in the neck. "Useless, useless," were the dying man's words. On July 7, the co-conspirators who had helped plan the attack and then sheltered the assassin were hanged in the courtyard of the penitentiary building in Washington.

BELOW **Lincoln spent his last hours lying unconscious in a dingy bed that was too small for his tall frame. There was nothing any doctor could do.**

HITS AND MISSES

James A. Garfield had only been in the oval office for four months when Charles J. Guiteau shot him on July 2, 1881. Two shots from a Webley revolver smashed into the president's back and right arm. Infection soon set in and Garfield passed away on September 19, 1881. His assassin, a lawyer, was hanged nine months later.

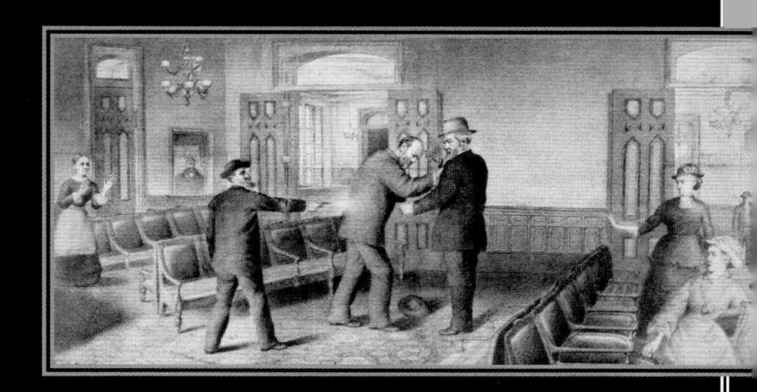

ABOVE **An artist's portrayal of the assassination of President James A. Garfield in 1881.**

William McKinley was shot by an anarchist named Leon Czolgosz on Friday, September 6, 1901, in New York. Czolgosz approached the president with a revolver concealed in a bandage around his arm. He let loose two shots and it appears that the second shot, which lodged in the president's gut, was the mortal wound. Garfield died seven days later. Czolgosz was sentenced to die in the electric chair and died in Auburn Prison on October 29, 1901. This assassination led to the secret service being given the role of protecting the president.

President Ford should have bought a lottery ticket during the month of September 1975. It was obviously a lucky time for him as he survived two assassination attempts. On September 5, a former follower of Charles Manson, Lynette 'Squeaky' Fromme, drew a pistol while standing close to the president. The gun failed to fire. On September 22, Sara Jane Moore took a shot with a recently bought handgun. She did not understand the sighting mechanism and narrowly missed Ford. Both women were sentenced to life imprisonment for their efforts.

President Andrew Jackson was fortunate to survive two shots as well. Both of these were on the same day—January 30, 1835. Richard Lawrence was somewhat unbalanced and believed he was King Richard the Third, the fifteenth-century English king. As Jackson walked out of the Capitol building, Lawrence pulled a pistol out of his coat. It misfired and the president ran at him and assaulted him with his cane. Lawrence pulled a second pistol out of his coat and pulled the trigger while aiming it into the president's stomach. It too misfired. Lawrence spent the rest of his days in a mental asylum.

Final Intermission

If two bullets are reputed to have changed world history, they would be either the ones that slammed into Archduke Franz Ferdinand's jugular and his wife's abdomen, or those that smashed into Pyotr Stolypin's arm and chest as he stood for intermission at the Kiev Opera House.

Even as he traveled with Czar Nicholas's entourage toward Kiev in that fateful month of September, 1911, Stolypin had a gut feeling that he would die there and never return to St. Petersburg. He was right, and with his death the ability of the Romanov dynasty to weather the oncoming storms died, too.

Stolypin was the outstanding figure of his generation. A large man with a dominant personality, he was able to use his vast stores of charisma to bend Russian society to his will. Appointed prime minister after the 1905 revolution, he was the superb practitioner of that old political skill, the carrot and the stick. Using his executive powers, the Okhrana (Russian secret police) was strengthened and revolutionaries around the country were hunted down. Sent to Siberia or hanged in their thousands with the "Stolypin neck tie," revolutionaries found there was nowhere to hide. At the same time the prime minister protected workers' rights, allowed peasants to buy their land, and brought in admirable social reforms such as free education and unemployment insurance. Within two years, it seemed the economy was thriving, and Nicholas was secure on his throne again.

Stolypin knew, though, that there was more work to be done. The chaotic financial system needed fixing, and ministries had to be improved to make them more efficient. Most importantly, Stolypin urged Nicholas to remain aloof from escalating tensions in Europe. He prophesied correctly that Russia was not ready for a war and wanted at least another decade to strengthen industry and the army. His advice was not followed, however, because in 1911 he was assassinated.

On September 1 of that year, Stolypin attended a performance at the Kiev Opera House. Seated at the front, just beyond the music pit, he seemed to be enjoying

LEFT **At the Kiev City Theater the Tsar witnessed the assassination of his effective Prime Minister Stolypin.**

himself immensely. During the second intermission, he stood up and was chatting with friends and associates when a young man dressed in evening clothes entered the theatre, passed the Okhrana security detail, and approached Stolypin with a determined gait. Stolypin noticed the young man and seemed about to ask him his business when the assassin drew a revolver and fired two shots point-blank at the prime minister. One shot smashed his right hand while the other tore into his chest. Pandemonium broke out as Stolypin sank into his seat. He tried to stand again, opened his coat to where the blood was pouring out over his finery, looked up at the Czar, and made the sign of the cross.

The assassin, Dmitry Bogrov, a young anarchist agitator and Okhrana informer, was arrested and almost beaten to death by the enraged operagoers.

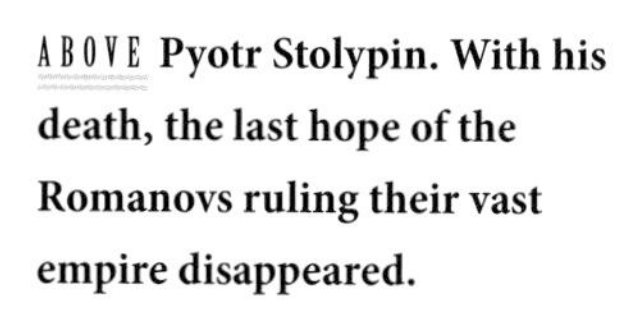

ABOVE **Pyotr Stolypin. With his death, the last hope of the Romanovs ruling their vast empire disappeared.**

The mortally wounded prime minister was rushed to the Makovsky Hospital, where he survived for another four days. Initially, it seemed he might pull through, and the doctors reported that his pulse was steady and he had not lost too much blood. However, on the third day, Stolypin took a turn for the worse. He became delirious as blood began to fester and rot from his damaged kidney and spleen. With his dying breath he uttered "Finland", followed by a last command: "Turn on the light." There were no lights where he was going, and Stolypin breathed his last.

Throughout Russia, the population went into shock. Stocks plummeted, and church attendance soared. Revolutionaries such as Lenin were delighted; they knew now the counterrevolution was over, and Nicholas would display all of his incompetence in the years to come. They were right. The one man who could hold the empire together was dead.

Nicholas and Alexandra did not attend the funeral. Rasputin disapproved of Stolypin, and it was under his influence that Stolypin was beginning to fall out of royal favor. Stolypin's killer was hanged after a suspiciously brief trial.

Death of a Peacemaker

Just as Mohandas Karamchand Gandhi tried to change history, it was the ideals of the past history of India that led to his assassination.

Nathuram Godse was the man who killed Gandhi. He was a member of a fanatical Hindu nationalist party. Hindu extremists such as Godse ignored 1,400 years of history and wanted to return India to a pure Hindu state. Ever since the rise of Islam in the 7th century CE, large portions of India had been dominated by Muslims. As the British Empire imploded, sectarian violence between the Hindu majority and the Muslim minority had been intensifying. The plan to separate India into Muslim Pakistan and Hindu India enraged Godse and his ilk. He decided to take Gandhi out.

Gandhi was born in 1869 in Porbandar, western India. Born into a family that played an active role in government, he went to London to study law when he turned 19. In pursuit of a legal career, he made his way to Natal in South Africa. Here he found a system of institutionalized racism. Whites were the dominant members of society, and other races were held in differing degrees of legal subjection. The native blacks were the most disadvantaged in society but Indians and Asians were not much better off. For 20 years Gandhi led nonviolent protests against the authorities. Returning to India in 1915, he became the dominant figure in the National Congress movement and was a vocal advocate of "home rule." He developed his civil disobedience campaign, which involved nonviolent noncooperation with the British. The British did not always reply in kind, and during the Amritsar massacre, 400 of his supporters were gunned down by British troops.

Gandhi's belief in nonviolent protest and his unceasing campaign against the

LEFT **This portrait of Ghandi was taken in the early 1940s at the height of his protest movement against British rule in India.**

RIGHT The conspirators, with Gandhi's killer, Nathuram Godse, sitting on the left next to some of his co-accused.

British Raj led to him being named "Mahatma"—"the Great Soul." After many stints in jail and unceasing protest, Gandhi and his movement forced the British cabinet to relinquish control of India on August 15, 1947. Gandhi described this as "the noblest act of the British nation." But it did not solve India's problem, and the subcontinent seemed to be descending into anarchy and violence. Gandhi began fasting to draw attention to the nation's plight and the need for moderation. It seemed to be working—but it was his last political act.

On the evening of January 30, 1948, Gandhi was walking with his nieces across the grounds of Birla House to attend to his evening devotions. As usual, Gandhi was only wearing his homespun *dhoti* and leaning on his staff. In a remarkable act of faith, he eschewed a bodyguard, although about 1,000 supporters flocked around him. As he approached the pagoda, Godse was waiting with a small caliber pistol concealed between his palms, which were arranged as if he was praying. As *bapu* ("father") came in range, Godse aimed the pistol and shot three bullets into his target.

Gandhi collapsed but seemed to raise his hands to his forehead in the Hindu gesture of forgiveness. Some reports say that he uttered "Hey Ram" (Oh God), while other witnesses believe that he said nothing at all. Godse then turned the pistol on himself, but one of the outraged witnesses knocked the pistol aside, and the Hindu fanatic only managed to graze his scalp with the fourth bullet.

After these shocking events, Prime Minister Jawaharlal Nehru announced to the watching press and to the world: "The light has gone out of our lives."

The day after his death, Gandhi's body was paraded through the streets of New Delhi surrounded by hundreds of thousands of mourning Indians. Both Hindus and Muslims turned out to grieve his loss. The funeral precession stretched for 5 miles (8 kilometers) before he was cremated on the banks of the sacred Jumna River.

It was found that eight other men were involved in the conspiracy to kill Gandhi. The two key conspirators, Godse and Narayan Apte, were hanged for the murder of the "Mahatma" on November 15, 1949. As a result, Hindu Nationalist parties were banned for the next ten years. To This day, "Father Gandhi" remains revered throughout the nation.

A Coup Gone Wrong

Ngo Dinh Diem was president of South Vietnam from October 1955 to his death on November 2, 1963. He and his brother were butchered in the back of an American-supplied APC (armored personnel carrier) by members of the South Vietnamese military who had been paid in US dollars to mount a coup. His death was much regretted by the American President Kennedy, who had merely wanted Diem removed from power.

Diem was appointed as the puppet president of South Vietnam by the Americans for three reasons: He hated the Communists, he was Christian, and he was known in the American Foreign Affairs Department. That he was incompetent and corrupt, and had poor judgment and a small base of support in South Vietnam was disregarded, with unfortunate results.

The Geneva Peace Accords, which guaranteed free and fair elections to reunify Vietnam, were ignored by Diem (probably with good reason, as the Communists were likely to win) and in the 1955 elections Diem's regime received 98 percent of the vote. Such was his success that he obtained 600,000 votes in Saigon, although only 450,000 people were registered!

Diem was a fanatic Catholic and used violence against the Cao Dai, Hoa Hao, and Buddhist organizations, driving many of their supporters into the arms of the Communists. He outlawed divorce, abortions, prostitution, and the use of opium while setting several of his brothers up as semi-autonomous warlords. Another brother was made the Vietnamese archbishop, while some members of the family were given prestigious highly paid roles within the government. Land was given to Catholic peasants fleeing from the North, but in the main he did not implement any meaningful land reform. In 1960, 45 percent of the land was owned by 2 percent of the population.

BELOW **President Ngo Dinh Diem, who managed to alienate almost the entire South Vietnamese population. The Americans were forced to remove him.**

Two policies proved catastrophic for Diem. By 1962 he had moved hundreds of thousands of peasants into "strategic hamlets," uprooting them from their ancestral lands and placing them within fortified villages so that Communists could not infiltrate the rural communities. This was carried out in an extremely ham-fisted manner, removing communities from the graves of their ancestors and destroying many hundreds of years of traditions. The second move was to ban the flying of Buddhist flags on

ABOVE **Thích Quảng Đức's self-immolation in 1963 alerted the world's media to the corruption, nepotism, and incompetence of the Diem regime.**

the Buddha's birthday. Troops loyal to the regime opened fire on protesting monks and civilians, escalating a minor point of order into a program of civil disobedience.

This may have remained a local issue only but on June 11, 1963, a 66-year-old monk, Thích Quảng Đức, adopted the lotus prayer position, doused himself with petrol, and set himself alight. Images of the monk flashed around the world even as Diem's powerful sister-in-law Madame Nhu (otherwise known as the dragon lady) hoped for more "barbecues" and police continued to raid Buddhist monasteries.

South Vietnam overflowed with riots in universities and high schools. Diem would not compromise, and by August 1963 the Kennedy administration decided that he had to go. Cable 243 was sent to the US ambassador, instructing him to seek out new leadership options, while CIA operatives encouraged a group of officers, led by Duong Van Minh, with cash handouts to organize a coup. Kennedy was complicit in the plot but sought assurances that the Diem clique would not be harmed in the coup.

Minh led the coup on November 1, 1963. Some officers remained loyal to Diem and his brother, Ngo Dinh Nhu, but they were soon dispatched with a bullet to the back of the head before being tumbled into makeshift graves at Tan Son Nhut airbase, the headquarters of the coup leaders. Meanwhile, despite assurances of safe passage, the two brothers had fled. Minh sent his two hatchet men, Captain Nguyen Van

Nhung and Major Duong Hieu Nghia, to "solve the problem." They set out in an armed convoy composed of several jeeps and M113 APCs. As his men left, Minh allegedly held up two fingers, indicating perhaps that he expected the two fugitives to be shot.

Nhung and Nghia did not have to be told twice. The next day, November 2, the brothers were seized in a church in Cholon district. They were bundled into the APC, Diem and Nhu on one side facing Nhung and Nghia on the other. As the convoy rattled through Saigon, it was held up at a railway crossing. Bystanders heard several men's voices coming from the APC, raised in a furious argument. This soon ended when the sound of pistol and semiautomatic fire echoed from the APC. While it is not entirely clear what happened, both brothers were shot and stabbed repeatedly.

Major Nghia gave an account in his official report. According to him, Captain Nhung and Diem's brother, Nhu, began to insult each other. The exchange became heated, and all manner of profanities were exchanged. The two men had enjoyed an acrimonious relationship for many years, and pent-up hatred was released in an incandescent screaming match. Diem sat silent through it all, according to Nghia. He perhaps saw what was going down.

Nhung had the excuse he wanted, and he pulled out his bayonet and leapt onto Nhu, stabbing him repeatedly—up to 26 times. Bloodied and panting, he turned from his first victim, pulled out a revolver, and shot the president in the head. He then turned to Nhu, saw he was still twitching, and shot him in the head, too.

Obviously Nghia wanted to cast blame elsewhere. But a press report came up with a different theory—that in fact Nghia had begun the killing by shooting both brothers at point-blank range, then Nhung sprayed them with a semiautomatic before stabbing them repeatedly.

Both stories have undeniable flaws. It is probably not a good idea to fire a semi-automatic machine gun in the confines of an APC, where shots can ricochet with deadly consequences, and it is unlikely that only one of Minh's hatchet men took part. Both accounts agree, though, that the two brothers did not put up a fight—their hands were bound behind their backs. None of those involved were charged with murder.

Minh became the new ruler of South Vietnam but was deposed on January 30, 1964. He was also the last president, albeit for only a few days, before Saigon fell to North Vietnam in 1975. Meanwhile, the government became a revolving door of corrupt politicians and military leaders, each one making it harder and harder for America to argue that they were anything other than puppets.

Diem may not have been a perfect ruler but at least he was a "conviction" politician who carried out some positive reforms. The North Vietnamese politburo saw his assassination as the beginning of the end of the US-backed regime.

A Warm Day in Dallas

The assassination of John F. Kennedy on November 22, 1963, was without doubt one of the most significant events of the 20th century. When he took office as US president in January 1961, with his beautiful and glamorous wife, Jacqueline, as First Lady, a new optimism swept through America, and it seemed the country was entering a new golden age. Surrounded by young advisors who were challenging the older generation, the new government was nicknamed "Camelot" in reference to the glory of a mythical King Arthur's court. Not only Americans but her allies around the world seemed caught up in the excitement of the handsome new president's term. This dream ended tragically.

The assassination took place while Kennedy was paying an official fund-raising visit to the city of Dallas, Texas. He had been advised by senior security officials and some of his aides to delay the visit, which had been preceded by many protests against politicians, as well as whispers of violence. In particular, his security

BELOW **President Kennedy in the limousine in Dallas, Texas, on Main Street, minutes before the assassination.**

advisors were reluctant to let him ride in an open-topped limousine in a location with so many potential sniping positions. The president had amassed a fair swag of enemies, including the Mafia, the Soviets, and the Cubans.

However, everything seemed to be going well—but when the cavalcade passed the Texas School Book Depository at approximately 12:30 p.m., three shots were fired from an Italian-made rifle.

Jeff Franzen was a six-year-old kid when he saw JFK assassinated directly in front of him. He and his parents had made their way to downtown Dallas to see the president and his motorcade. Jeff was upset with being hauled out of home. To sweeten the deal, his mother had brought him a ball to play with, but minutes before the arrival of the presidential cavalcade it had disappeared down a drain. In the fullness of time the little boy might have forgotten about that ball, but what happened next would be seared on his memory. For some reason the motorcade had slowed down, and the family were standing on the curb right next to the road as it approached when they heard what sounded like three firecrackers going off. Jeff saw what he thought was confetti being thrown from the presidential car; it was in fact fragments of the president's brain.

He had witnessed the effect of the second of two shots that hit the president. Of the three shots fired, one missed. The first to hit the

BELOW **The festive atmosphere of Kennedy's motorcade is obvious in this photo. Also obvious is the lack of effective security.**

KENNEDY AND GOVERNOR CONNALLY BOTH LAY BLEEDING AS THE CAR SPED OFF TO THE NEAREST HOSPITAL—PARKLAND MEMORIAL—WHILE THEIR WIVES DID THEIR BEST TO KEEP THEIR HUSBANDS ALIVE UNTIL THEY ARRIVED.

president entered his back and exited just above the collar bone. Kennedy slumped forward. This first shot, the "magic bullet," ricocheted into Texas Governor John Connally and the wound could have been mortal, were it not for the governor's wife. She pulled her husband down into cover and at the same time limited the blood loss from his wounds.

The second shot that hit Kennedy was mortal. It smashed chunks of flesh, skull, and brain matter from his head and on to the trunk of the large convertible sedan. Abraham Zapruder's famous 8mm footage of the incident shows Jacqueline Kennedy scrambling out of her seat onto the rear hood of the vehicle as if she is trying to escape the gunman's deadly fire. In fact, she was not thinking of her own well-being. The president's wife was desperately trying to grab pieces of her husband's brain and skull, as if she could somehow repair the damage that had been done. She gathered up the bloody stuff, before retreating back into the sedan. Security details swarmed over the vehicle, but it was too late. One of the security detail shielding the first lady looked at JFK's head but saw only bloody braincase.

The reaction from the crowd was mixed. Some thought a car had backfired. People closer to the scene knew something was desperately wrong. As the president's car accelerated away, motorcycle cops suddenly descended on the scene. One crashed right in front of the Franzen family. Jeff's father, an ex-serviceman, realized there was a gunman on the loose; he pitched his wife and child to the ground and covered them with his body. Elsewhere, people were running around frantically, and the wave of cheering that had accompanied the car to this point changed to a terrified roar. Only one civilian was injured: James Tague was hit by concrete debris, possibly dislodged from the road by the first bullet, which had missed its target.

Kennedy and Governor Connally both lay bleeding as the car sped off to the nearest hospital—Parkland Memorial—while their wives did their best to keep their husbands alive until they arrived. As Connally exhaled, a bloody mist emerged from his mouth, evidence of the dreadful internal damage he had sustained.

When the president arrived at the hospital, it was clear to staff that he was not going to survive, and a priest was called to administer the last rites. Meanwhile, Governor Connally was undergoing emergency surgery and eventually pulled

ABOVE **Frightened spectators, perhaps including Jeff Franz and his family, hug the ground moments after a sniper's bullet strikes President Kennedy.**

through. His wife's prompt action of pulling him to her lap in the car so the wound in his chest was able to close up had helped save his life. Had she not done so, he would have almost certainly bled to death.

By the time the priest arrived, Kennedy was dead. A nurse on the scene later reported that it seemed as if his whole cerebral cavity was blown out. His eyes were still wide open, startled as if he had just received a surprise. He had no hope once the second bullet hit. As the priest was intoning the last rites over the president's body in Trauma Ward One, Jacqueline came to bid farewell to her husband. She swapped rings and gave him one last kiss.

Once the president was declared dead, his body was taken from the hospital and straight to the presidential airplane. This was against required procedure—as the president had been murdered, there should have been a full forensic examination by the coroner in order to determine the exact cause of death before the corpse was returned to the family. This decision to remove the body so rapidly helped the conspiracy theorists who would soon begin dissecting the events of the assassination. The plane flew to Washington, DC, where an incompetent autopsy was performed at Bethesda Naval Hospital. The results were not recorded properly, further muddying the waters.

In America, and indeed in much of the Western world, confusion and shock followed the news of the cold-blooded killing. Some military and national guard formations were mobilized in case the hit was a prelude to an attack on America by the USSR and her allies.

On a more personal level, many students were dismissed from school early, shops were closed, and complete strangers hugged each other on the streets. People from that generation inevitably remember exactly where they were that day, just as

BELOW The news of the assassination raced around the world. Here, a horrified crowd listens for news outside a radio shop.

ABOVE **The Texas School Book Depository in Dallas is maintained as a monument to the dead president. Oswald's sniper's nest is preserved as he left it.**

those who witnessed 9/11 know what they were doing at the time the planes hit the Twin Towers.

The media went into a frenzy. On the day of Kennedy's funeral, November 25, a national day of mourning was declared, and thousands thronged to see the president's coffin. Heads of state from more than 90 countries were present at the funeral.

Meanwhile, the hunt for the killer was on. It was soon clear that the most likely source of the shots was the nearby Texas School Book Depository. Police swarmed into the building, and a roll call was taken of the employees. Only one man was missing: Lee Harvey Oswald. He had made his escape and walked into a cinema. An abandoned rifle and firing post were found.

A police officer thought that the suspicious-looking character who had entered the cinema could be a likely culprit and had radioed for backup. Oswald was pulled down by a swarm of police. They were sure they had got their man, and made sure the public knew it too—Oswald was paraded outside the sheriff's office up to 15 times so the press could get a good look at him. His palm print was found on the abandoned weapon.

Approximately a week after the killing, the Warren Commission was set up to discover the exact cause of Kennedy's death. The commission ultimately found that the trained shooter, Lee Harvey Oswald, had loosed off the bullets that killed the Kennedy dream. Initially, these findings were derided. Conspiracy theorists were particularly skeptical of the "magic bullet" that passed through Kennedy's throat before maiming the Texas governor sitting in front of him. Many thought, and still think, that another gunman on "the grassy knoll" must have fired as well. However, recent forensic and ballistic testing has supported the Warren Commission's original findings.

As it turned out, the assassin Lee Harvey Oswald had a history of mental illness, and also had links to the Soviet Union. He was born in New Orleans on October 18, 1939. His father died shortly after he was born, and his mother sent him packing to a children's home when he was three years old. Later, when his mother remarried, he rejoined the family, but as a teenager he showed severe behavior problems. As a young man, he became a Marxist. He served abroad in the US Marines, and after his discharge he visited the USSR, where he applied to become a citizen. When this request was rejected by the authorities, he attempted suicide and was then allowed to stay in the country. He married a Russian girl, had a child, and then moved back to the USA.

It seems that Oswald was keen to make his mark on history, and his wife claimed that he had made plans to assassinate a right-wing general, Edwin Walker. This came to nothing. The family moved to Dallas, and Lee Harvey got a job at the Texas School Book Depository. He fared quite well there but all the time he was planning another violent act. No doubt when Oswald heard of the president's visit and researched his itinerary, he decided it was time to act.

On the day of the assassination, Oswald went to work as usual and somehow smuggled in his rifle. As a trained shooter, he was able to set up a sniper's vantage point. He rested the scoped rifle on several boxes filled with books as a solid mount to shoot from. After letting off his three shots in rapid succession, he bolted from the building under cover of the confusion caused by the assassination. Soon after, Oswald

BELOW **Lee Harvey Oswald with his sniper's rifle, taken in Oswald's back yard in Dallas by Marina Oswald, his Russian wife.**

ABOVE **The president's mourning family leaves the Capitol in Washington after his funeral on November 25, 1963.**

was approached on the street by a police officer, J.D. Tippit. At this point he pulled out a gun and fired at the police officer several times before running away, leaving Tippit dying on the street. Helped by members of the public, other officers pursued the fugitive, and he was soon under arrest.

While the police were parading their suspect in front of the press on November 24, 1963, Jack Ruby, a Dallas nightclub owner, shot Oswald in the stomach from point-blank range. The assassin died soon afterward, too soon to go to trial and allow the whole truth of the situation to come out.

Another Televized Death

John F. Kennedy had only a fraction of a second of awareness between the moment when the first and then the second bullet slammed into his shoulder and head. The president's brother, Bobby Kennedy, was not so fortunate. Hit by a volley of explosive .22 caliber shells, he collapsed while still holding on to the last well-wisher to shake his hand. One of the first photos of the stricken Kennedy shows him lying on the ground, looking around while desperately trying to rise and resume his life—scarcely able to comprehend that his life is over.

He asks "Is everybody OK?" as people cluster around him. The next photographs show his left eye closing as his brain begins to shut down. The other eye remains open, full of fear as he acknowledges his plight.

On June 5, 1968, Kennedy—who was seeking nomination as the Democratic presidential candidate for the November elections—was gunned down by a Palestinian named Sirhan Sirhan while walking through the kitchen of the Ambassador Hotel in Los Angeles. Sirhan Sirhan claimed that he was acting in revenge of Democrat support for Israel during the Six-Day War. Whatever his motive, he easily penetrated Bobby Kennedy's small security detail (a retired detective and two professional athletes) and fired a succession of shots at point-blank range.

The assassin used a .22 eight-shot Iver-Johnson revolver, and he managed to empty the gun before being thrown to the floor. Five bystanders were hit but the shots that struck Kennedy wounded him mortally. The bullets fired were "mini mag" lead hollow points, which mushroom on impact. The key advantage for an assassin is that once they have impacted the target they bloom outward and fragment, causing maximum internal damage while rarely exiting and striking bystanders.

The mortal shot hit Bobby Kennedy's skull just behind the right ear and tore into his brain. Initially, blood poured from the entry wound before clotting, causing the blood to leak into the cranial cavity. The traumatized brain tissue began to swell and this, as well as the blood accumulating in the inter-cranial space, began to exert pressure on the parts of the brain regulating heart and lung functions. If the pressure had not been released, he would have died in minutes; however, a doctor, Stanley Abo, rushed to give aid and recognized that the pressure building within the skull could be fatal. He stuck his finger in the wound and cleared the clot. Blood poured out again—a mixed blessing at best.

The wounded man was transported to the Good Samaritan Hospital, where surgeons operated in a desperate attempt to save his life. He had been shot three

RIGHT **From left to right: Robert Kennedy, Ted Kennedy, and John Kennedy in happier times. Only Ted would avoid an assassin's bullet.**

times. Two bullets entered the rear of his right armpit; one exited through his chest wall, while the other remained in the back of his neck. The fatal shot was the one that entered behind the right ear—it pushed smashed bone into his brain and dispersed fragments of the bullet throughout his head.

Neurosurgeons tried desperately to extract the fragments, but it was an impossible task, and Kennedy died more than 24 hours after the shooting.

Death of a Dynasty

Indira Gandhi's security seemed assured. The Indian prime minister lived in a huge walled compound in the heart of New Delhi. A high stone fence lined with large trees surrounded the secure area, preventing any observers looking into the compound from adjacent buildings. Two gates that allowed access into the prime ministerial residence and office were guarded 24/7 by heavily armed guards. Uniformed police were stationed at intervals around the perimeter, while security personnel circling the compound in unmarked cars established an around-the-clock security cordon. But Indira was not to be assassinated by outside attackers. She fell to the bullets of those who were meant to protect her.

The future prime minister was born in 1917 in Allahabad, India. She was the daughter of Jawaharlal Nehru, who became the first prime minister of independent India. She was educated at Oxford University, where she showed an early interest in politics. Returning to India in the late 1930s, the young

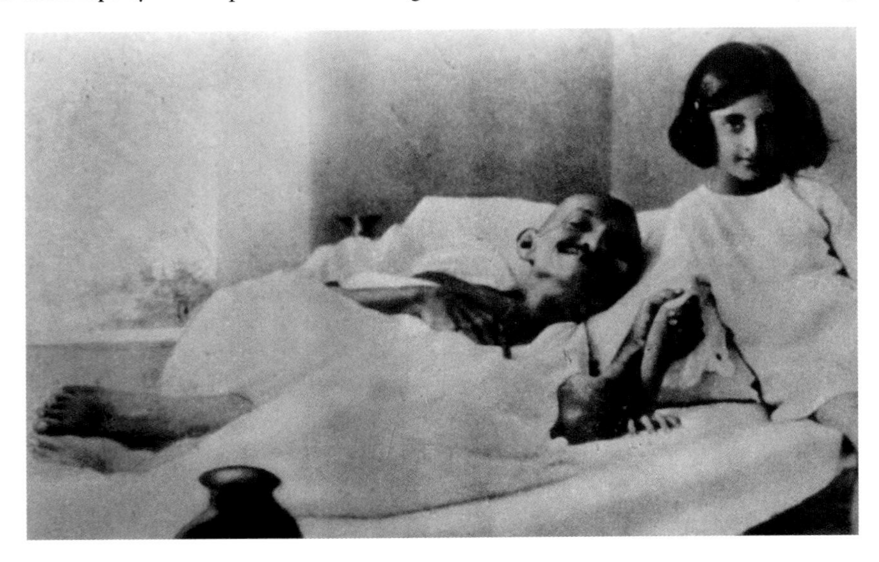

BELOW **Young Indira Nehru with Mahatma Gandhi during his fast in 1924. While not related, she was closely associated with his party.**

ABOVE Indian Prime Minister Indira Gandhi and US President Lyndon B. Johnson meeting in the Oval Office of the White House, 1966.

politician joined the Indian congress and was imprisoned for some time by the English rulers.

In 1942, she married Feroze Gandhi. Feroze was a journalist and was not in any way related to the revered "Mahatma" Gandhi. Sitting in parliament, Indira was propelled into the role of prime minister in 1966. The Congress Party thought she would be easy to dominate, but she proved to be as strong-willed as her father.

It was this strong will that was to be her downfall. India and neighboring Sri Lanka are countries made up of many different religious and racial groups. During the 1960s and 70s, many separatist movements arose where different peoples sought autonomy. Indira encouraged the Tamils in Sri Lanka by funding the terrorist movement there, but at the same time she ruthlessly squashed dissent in India.

In the Punjab, the proud Sikh peoples sought autonomy. At first, Indira sought some type of compromise with moderate Sikhs, but this failed, and separatist extremists occupied the Golden Temple at Amritsar. The prime minister was having none of it and on June 1, 1984 ordered Operation Blue Star. For eight days, the Indian military, backed up with tanks, helicopters, artillery, and crack commando units, assaulted this most holy of Sikh shrines.

Thousands from both sides were killed or wounded, and throughout the countryside Sikh military units rebelled. Despite this, the separatists' radical leader, Sant Jarnail Singh Bhindranwale, was killed in the assault, and the movement was all but crushed. But Indira Gandhi had signed her own death warrant.

ABOVE **The sacred Sikh Golden Temple. Ghandi's order for a massive military assault on this temple led to her assassination.**

Within her bodyguard were several Sikhs. For hundreds of years, Sikhs, known for their bright turbans and bushy beards, had established a reputation for bravery and loyalty second to none. Beant Singh and Satwant Singh were trusted guards within the prime minister's inner circle. Beant had served his mistress for ten years, and she held him in esteem and affection. After the crackdown at the Golden Temple, Indira had been advised to move these guards to other duties. The prime minister refused on several grounds, one being that it would further erode her image as a tolerant secular figure.

She should have listened to her security chief's warnings. On October 31, 1984, at 8:30 a.m., Indira left her residence within the secure compound to walk the 200 yards to her offices. The stately gardens abounded with water features, hedges, and gracefully sculpted flower beds. At one stage she had to pass through a gap in a hedge, and while her main bodyguard trailed behind, the two Singhs stood to attention on either side of the entrance. The prime minister greeted them with a smile and the courteous gesture of folded hands and a slight bow. She whispered "Namaste," the traditional statement of good will.

Beant Singh drew his .38 British issue Webley and fired three shots into the prime minister's abdomen. As she collapsed onto the gravel path, Satwant Singh pulled his Sten submachine gun off his shoulder, cocked the magazine, and aimed at the stricken woman. Sten guns were notorious for jamming but this wasn't the case with Satwant's. He pumped the full 30 rounds into Indira. Seven went into her guts, three into the chest, and at least one straight through her heart.

The two dropped their guns as the security detail seized them. "I've done what I had to do, you do what you have to do," Beant said to his captors. As the assassins were dragged toward the guardhouse, they too received a hail of submachine gunfire. It was probably a classic case of "shot while trying to escape," but the guards said that Beant had changed his mind and lunged for one of his captors' Sten guns, earning him and his co-conspirator a belly full of lead. Beant died immediately; Satwant survived to be hanged on January 6, 1989.

Doctors tried desperately to save the shot woman. In the All India Institute of Medical Sciences Hospital, she was given at least 88 bottles of blood, even though she was probably DOA. A wave of anti-Sikh sentiment swept the country, and a conservative estimate places the death toll at 3,000 individuals as they were pulled off trains and beaten to death or incinerated in Sikh temples.

Rajiv Gandhi was Indira's younger son. He had been reluctant to enter politics, but with the death of his brother in a plane crash he was the only one who could fulfill his mother's wish for a dynasty of Nehrus to rule India. He assumed the role of prime minister on his mother's death and continued many of her policies. One he did not pursue was her funding of the separatist Tamil Tigers in Sri Lanka. In 1987 he made peace with the war-torn country and sent 50,000 Indian soldiers to help quell the Tamil revolt.

In 1991, Rajiv was campaigning for re-election. He visited a temple in the rural town of Sriperumbudur, southwest of Madras (Chennai). Ten thousand well-wishers greeted him, and many lined up on a red carpet to pay their respects. A Tamil woman in a red wig approached Rajiv, handed him a posy, and bowed deeply. As she bowed, she pressed a detonation switch on her chest. She became a flaming fireball as five sticks of cyclotrimethylenetrinitramine strapped to her torso and packed with steel pellets and ball bearings exploded. Her head was flung 330 feet (100 meters) away into the press gallery, while Rajiv's face was blown off and his torso shredded. Seventeen other people died within the blast radius, and hundreds lay wounded.

The Tamil Tigers had struck. They had been nurtured by Rajiv's mother, and his betrayal of their cause led to an explosive payback.

Sonia Gandhi—Rajiv's wife—was offered the prime ministership by Congress. For some reason, she refused…

Angels of Anger, Fire, and Death

October 1995. It's the eve of Yom Kippur, one of the most sacred days in the Jewish calendar, and a group of fanatical right-wing Israelis gather outside the home of their prime minister to deliver an ancient curse used for thousands of years to damn the enemies of Israel. The curse is aptly named Pulsa D'Nura ("lashes of fire"). They intone:

> *"I give to you, the angels of anger, fire, and death, Yitzhak, son of Rosa Rabin—thus you may smother him, make him into a wraith. Make him sick so that he is confined, take his wealth, trouble his thoughts and send Yitzhak mad so that he wastes away and dies. Put the curse on Yitzhak Rabin and DAMN HIM, DAMN HIM, DAMN HIM..."*

One month later, Yitzhak died—not through a slow wasting away or a descent into madness, but in a hail of bullets fired by a fanatical Zionist assassin. With the death of Rabin, the last chance of a lasting peace between the Palestinian Arabs and the Jewish citizens of the State of Israel may have passed. Rabin and the Palestinian leader Yasser Arafat were on the verge of signing a proclamation that would perhaps have allowed the two peoples to coexist peacefully. The bullets fired by Yigal Amir put an end to that dream and may even have contributed to dire situation in the Middle East today.

Looking at Prime Minister Yitzhak Rabin's early life, many observers wondered why he earned such hatred from some of his people. He was in every way a true Israeli hero. Zionism is a Jewish nationalist movement that believes in the creation and defense of a Jewish nationalist state in Palestine, the ancient homeland of the biblical Jews. Rabin, born in March 1922, came from an impeccable Zionist background. His mother, Rosa,

LEFT **Lieutenant Colonel Yitzhak Rabin in the War of Independence. A fierce fighter for the foundation of Israel, he later tried to accommodate the Palestinian needs.**

ABOVE Nobel Peace Prize Laureates Yasser Arafat, Shimon Peres, and Yitzhak Rabin, in Oslo, 1994. The fragile peace was broken with the death of Rabin.

was one of the most important Zionist leaders of her time. She dedicated her entire life to the establishment of a Jewish homeland, and although it seems Yitzhak was sometimes neglected by his mother, he embraced her passionate ideology.

As soon as he was able, the future prime minister enrolled in the Palmach, an elite commando unit of the Haganah, the Zionist militia. He soon rose through the ranks and in 1948 was appointed commander of the 1,400 men of the newly formed Harel Brigade. When the UN proclaimed the partition of Palestine into a Muslim territory and a Jewish state, the neighboring Arab powers sought to invade the new Israeli territories and overwhelm them. One of the fiercest formations facing the Haganah was the 10,000-strong Arab Legion. Rabin's brigade of three battalions was charged with the relief of Old Jerusalem and the protection of the 90,000 Jews living in the area. His units fought heroically against many formations, including elements of the Arab Legion. They suffered tremendous casualties and after several weeks were down to two-thirds of their original strength. Despite some setbacks, Rabin fought tenaciously and seized the old town, as well as the sacred Mount Zion.

In battle against the Arabs (and, before that, the British), Rabin proved himself to be a daring and courageous fighter. But he also took part in the expulsion of some 50,000 Palestinian residents from the towns of Lydda and Ramle, situated between Tel Aviv and Jerusalem. Several hundred villagers were shot during that operation, part of a wider exodus of Palestinians from the new Jewish state. Rabin had more than demonstrated his Zionist credentials.

BATH

Rabin added to these laurels (from an Israeli point of view) as the Chief of Staff of the IDF (Israel Defense Forces) in the 1967 Six-Day War. Surrounded by the hostile states of Egypt, Jordan, Syria, and Lebanon, the Israelis were outnumbered two to one in infantry, three to one in tanks and armored vehicles, and three to one in fighter planes. Despite this, Rabin sent in early air strikes that gave his troops overwhelming air superiority. The enemy forces were routed, suffering catastrophic losses of men and material. The Six-Day War made Rabin a national hero and left Israel in possession of the West Bank, Gaza, East Jerusalem, parts of Syria, and more than a million Palestinians.

Rabin traded in his military celebrity for a political career and was twice elected prime minister. His first period in office was from 1974 to 1977, and his second term began in 1992. He brought in many positive reforms, including a modern healthcare system and an up-to-date education system.

While these reforms played well domestically, Rabin also earned international praise for his role in the Oslo Peace Accords. Elected on a platform of reconciliation between Palestinians and Israelis, the prime minister acted with characteristic boldness and secretly met with his opponent, Yasser Arafat. The two men and their negotiating team thrashed out the Israel–Palestinian accords, which guaranteed that the Palestinians would be treated well and that Israel would withdraw from the occupied territories. The Palestinians were given self-governance, and the Gaza Strip and West Bank were to be returned to the original inhabitants.

Jewish settlements spreading within the occupied territories were, and still are, the main source of conflict between the two peoples. Many Jewish communities brutalized and seized land from the original inhabitants, building paramilitary compounds to hold on to the new territory. The peace accords were designed to stop this process and return the lands to their original owners. The American president Bill Clinton witnessed the signing of the peace accords between the two former antagonists on the White House lawns and the world breathed a sigh of relief. Maybe the savage wars and terrorist attacks caused by the conflict would cease.

It was not to be.

Yigal Amir was born in 1970 in the mainly Arab state of Yemen. He came from an orthodox Jewish family and as soon as possible the family immigrated to the new state of Israel. Like all young men at the time, he spent some years in compulsory military service. On completion, Amir became involved in right-wing politics while studying law at university. He became fanatically obsessed with the idea of spreading Orthodox Jewish religious practices throughout Israel and not returning any land to

LEFT **Chief of Staff Lt. Gen. Yitzhak Rabin (left) in the entrance to the old city of Jerusalem during the Six-Day War, with Moshe Dayan (center) and Uzi Narkiss (right).**

the Palestinians. He became a prime mover in several organizations and organized protests against the Oslo Accords, which he saw as a betrayal of the Zionist belief in a purely Jewish homeland occupying all of the lands of Palestine. The return of occupied territory to the Palestinian Arabs was anathema to Amir, and he was determined to stop the process.

The possibility of killing Rabin first occurred to Amir when he met the prime minister at a wedding of a close friend in Tel Aviv. He was amazed that security was so lax that any person with a pistol strapped into their belt could easily take out the politician. Once it was clear that the peace process was becoming more of a reality, Amir determined to take down Rabin. He purchased a Beretta semiautomatic and waited in a car park adjoining Tel Aviv square, where Rabin was attending a peace rally.

This peace rally was a spectacular triumph for Rabin. He had originally been reluctant to attend, as he thought that the ceaseless propaganda from the right-wing factions may have discredited the peace process. The opposite had occurred. More than 100,000 Israelis turned out to support their prime minister, totally dwarfing any rallies opposing the Oslo Accords. It seemed that most of the Israelis wanted the fighting to cease and to live in harmony with their Palestinian brothers.

Yigal Amir was not interested in peace. He wanted the conflict with the Palestinians to persist so that the Zionist land grab could continue. As Rabin walked to his car, Amir stepped out of the shadows and fired two shots into the prime minister's back. One of the bullets smashed into the old peacemaker's lung, destroying its structure and leading to massive hemorrhages and blood loss. Rabin was rushed to hospital but the internal damage was too severe. He died soon afterward.

Amir didn't resist arrest. He celebrated and asked his guards to join him in a toast with schnapps. He was taken into custody and received a life sentence for the atrocity. He never expressed remorse for his actions and even married a Jewish Russian, Larisa Trembovler, while in jail. He requested conjugal visits but they were denied.

LEFT **Israeli Yigal Amir, the assassin of Israeli Premier Yitzhak Rabin. He proposed a toast of schnapps to his guards after his arrest.**

Amir had often talked of his desire to kill the prime minister. He had railed against Rabin to relatives and friends. Even fellow students had put up with his rants and heard repeatedly that Amir wanted to assassinate Rabin. No action was taken against the radical right-wing ideologue. Either Israeli security forces ignored the threat, or else they only saw threats coming from Palestinian activists. Some evidence exists that they even colluded in the assassination.

Israeli security agencies have thrived since the assassination of Rabin. The peace process stalled, Israeli settlements in the West Bank have multiplied exponentially, and the conflict that was confined to the British protectorate of Palestine has spread into Iraq, Iran, Syria, Afghanistan, and Turkey.

It is possible that if the Oslo Accords had not been stymied, the Middle East would now be at peace. Two bullets made it impossible.

Death by Camera

Grainy footage exists of the aftermath of the Lion of Panjshir's assassination by Tunisian al-Qaeda suicide bombers. The camera moves into a large room filled with destroyed and still smoking furniture, lingering on a large upholstered chair in the center of the rear wall. It was here that Ahmad Shah Massoud was killed by explosives hidden in the battery pack and camera of a "journalist." The camera pans away from Massoud's chair to the right. Here, slouched against another wall, is the shattered torso of his assassin, thrown here when he detonated his suicide bomb. The other assassin was hunted down and shot.

Ahmad Shah Massoud's leadership was the last bastion against Taliban domination of Afghanistan. From 1996 to 2001, the Taliban, inspired by Mohammed Omar and funded by Saudi and Pakistani interests, had seized most of Afghanistan. With them they brought a strict interpretation of sharia law. Women were forbidden to work or gain an education. Men had to wear beards. Hands were hacked off for petty crimes, and all Western influences and entertainments were banned. Following the victorious "Talib" (religious students) was the infamous 055 Brigade responsible for countless massacres of innocent civilians. Osama Bin Laden had founded this group along with his terrorist network al-Qaeda, which swore death and destruction to all Westerners. At this stage, Bin Laden was a relatively minor figure, known only to intelligence networks.

By 2001, 90 percent of Afghanistan had fallen to the radical Islamist forces. Massoud and his Northern Alliance forces were dug in in several northern provinces, and at least 100,000 refugees had fled into his territory, seeking the more tolerant democratic forms of government he allowed. Massoud was born on September 2,

1953, and soon proved to be a gifted individual. Outraged at the 1979 Soviet invasion of Afghanistan, he raised a guerrilla force of mujahideen and soon proved to be a gifted and charismatic military leader. It was during this time he earned the name "Lion of Panjshir." When the Taliban sought to conquer Afghanistan, he was the last to hold out against the fundamentalist Muslims and he urgently sought assistance from foreign powers. None were forthcoming, and his forces had to battle the well-funded Taliban alone.

The Taliban knew that if they were to complete their conquest of Afghanistan, they would have to eliminate Massoud. Al-Qaeda wanted him gone too. Earlier that year, on a mission to raise international support in Europe, he had warned of an imminent terrorist attack. That attack is now known as 9/11.

The two assassins tasked with the mission to kill Massoud knew they were entering dangerous territory. There had been many attempts to kill the resistance fighter, the first when he was 22 years old. Warfare in Afghanistan is particularly savage. The fate of prisoners captured by either side is particularly blood-curdling.

Thirty-four-year-old Karim Touzani and 26-year-old Kacem Bakkali knew they were embarking on a suicide mission when they entered Afghanistan late in August 2001, seeking an interview with Massoud. They posed as members of the media, Touzani as the journalist and Bakkali as his photographer. Hindsight is a wonderful thing, and after the assassination, members of the Northern Alliance who had escorted the two men to Massoud's mountainous military base at Khwaja Bahauddin spoke of their strange behavior. They were extremely reluctant to be photographed and, unlike most journalists, rarely asked questions, even when they were on a tour of the front lines. One time Bakkali did speak out was when he asked the driver of their 4WD to slow down lest the jolting caused by the rough terrain should damage his camera.

Bakkali's concern for his camera was real. It was packed with plastic explosives, ready to detonate as soon as it was turned on. The battery pack he wore round his back was in reality a belt also packed with explosives. It was the two North African al-Qaeda members' plan to get close enough to Massoud so they could blow him and his entourage sky-high. Both men carried forged Moroccan passports. Both were al-Qaeda-trained Tunisians recruited from disenchanted Muslims in Belgium. (Touzani's real name was Abdelsattar Dahmane, and Bakkali's was Rachid Bourawi Alwaer.)

Once they arrived at the Northern Alliance's headquarters, they were stymied for three weeks in their attempts to get an interview. Finally, early on September 9, 2001, the two assassins were admitted into Massoud's presence as he was sitting down for a meal. In front of him was a small table laden with bread, cheese, almonds, and cream. He reached over the table to shake the hands of the two men. Bakkali asked if he could move the table before setting up his tripod-mounted camera so it was aimed directly at Massoud's chest.

The one survivor of the bombing recorded what happened next. Masood Khalili was acting as his commander's interpreter. The initial smiles of the journalist faded as he spat out his questions to Massoud. "Why do you hate Bin Laden and why do you accuse him of being a murderer?" Too late, Khalili noted the change in tone, and the room erupted into a fireball. The cameraman's legs were fragmented and his torso was thrown against the far wall. The explosion enveloped Massoud in flame and pieces of metal tore into his body. Two pieces of shrapnel, either from the explosive belt or from the remains of the camera, pierced his heart, giving him only a few short moments to live. Khalili saw blue fire racing at him, and in the spilt second before he lost consciousness, he thought a missile had hit the base.

ABOVE A picture of Ahmad Shah Massoud, the Lion of Panjshir, in front of his tomb in the Panjshir province of Afghanistan.

Massoud's most loyal bodyguard, Haji Mohammad Omar, rushed into the room and found everything on fire. His boss was still sitting in his plush chair, smoking and covered in blood. He picked Massoud up and, racing out of the smoldering compound, placed him in his armored command vehicle before racing toward the helicopter pad to take him for medical treatment, a scarce 10 minutes away. When they reached the Tajikistan medical clinic, life signs had ceased. The "Lion of Panjshir" was dead.

Two days later, Osama Bin Laden launched the second phase of his operation and slammed two jetliners into the Twin Towers.

Ironically, this strengthened the Northern Alliance. Two days after the largest terrorist attack in history, American military advisors arrived at Massoud's headquarters, promising unlimited military assistance to take out the Taliban and eliminate Osama Bin Laden. They were good for their word, and soon the Northern Alliance, with massed support from America and her allies, had retaken most of Afghanistan from the Taliban and sent Bin Laden into hiding.

Rebels and Revolutionaries

Nothing is stronger than the power of ideas. One man or woman can change the world if they can carry the population along with them and try to right thousands of wrongs. But those who seek to keep the world as it is and reinforce the status quo know there is one surefire way of keeping injustice alive—you have to "shoot the messenger." Many idealists, such as Thomas Becket and Martin Luther King, have tried to improve the lot of their fellow man. Many have died in the attempt.

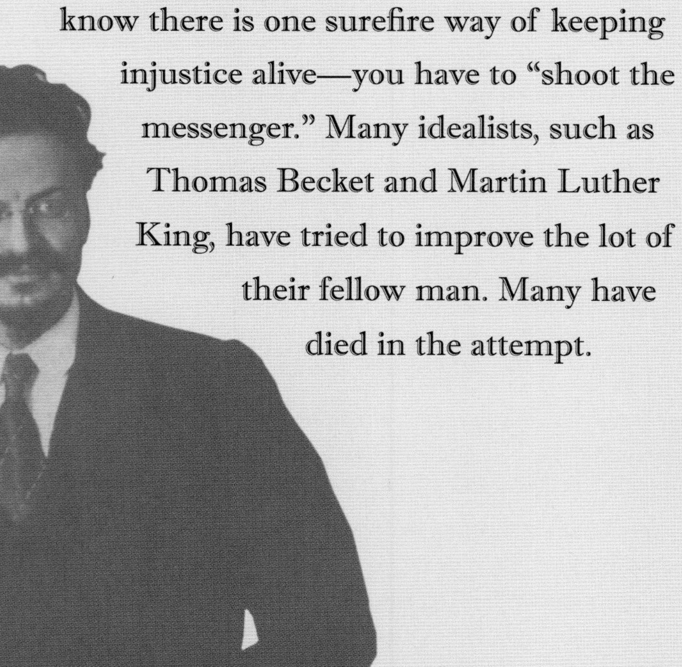

A Genius Dies

The commander of the Roman siege of Syracuse, Marcus Claudius Marcellus, ordered his men NOT to assassinate the Greek mathematical genius Archimedes. This was despite the fact that the siege of the Greek state, located on the east coast of Sicily, had ground on for two years, largely due to the sophisticated war machines engineered by Archimedes.

At the height of the Second Punic War (218–201 BCE), Syracuse's leaders broke their long alliance with Rome and supported the Carthaginians. In 214 BCE, Marcellus, at the head of approximately 20,000 men, laid siege to the well-fortified city.

Syracuse was already a hard nut to crack and had a deadly array of defensive siege engines. These included catapults that could hurl flaming fireballs hundreds of yards (meters) and onagers that could throw stones up to 700 mina (660 pounds/300 kilograms). Any of these could destroy a ship with one hit. On the landward side, Archimedes improved on already-imposing defenses and built gallery upon gallery dripping with powerful ballista. Some reports had these ballistas—basically early crossbow devices—firing multiple bolts up to 6 feet (1.83 meters) long. One bolt was reported to have skewered three Romans at once.

But while Archimedes' genius improved upon these existing devices, he also developed weapons that seem straight out of science fiction. The first "death ray" was devised when he arranged a series of mirrors that reflected the sun's rays and combined them into one concentrated stream, which ignited the rigging and sails on Roman warships. Another invention was the giant claw. The Romans mounted siege towers on some of their ships, and as a ship approached the city walls the Greeks grabbed its prow with a giant steel claw and, through an ingenious lever system, picked it up until it stood on its stern and then dropped it back into the water, causing it to break up or capsize.

BELOW Archimedes turned his phenomenal intellect to producing weapons of war. These included devices that could burn Roman ships using sunlight.

The Romans lost many men in costly frontal assaults, and after two years of bloody warfare they only managed to gain entry into the town through subterfuge: A small party of Roman troops infiltrated the town during a religious festival and let in the entire army. Marcellus gave specific orders to his troops to take Archimedes alive.

Like many great mathematicians and thinkers, it is likely that Archimedes was on the autistic spectrum, and this led to his death. At the very least he suffered from Asperger's and was not always able to read subtle and not-so-subtle signals given out by his peers. Even while the town around him was being sacked, the great mathematician was wholly absorbed in cracking mathematical calculations on the sandy floor of his house. When a Roman soldier burst in upon Archimedes and demanded loot, Archimedes flew at him, demanding that the Roman not disturb his workings—obviously misreading the rather obvious non-verbal cues given by the veteran armed killer. Either because he did not recognize the mathematician, or because he did and realized how many Roman deaths the genius was responsible for, the soldier grabbed the old man and slit his throat, pouring blood all over Archimedes' final solution.

LEFT **Thanks to Archimedes' inventive genius, the Syracusians were able to hold off the Roman assaults in the siege of 214 BCE.**

BELOW **The Roman commander Marcellus ordered that Archimedes had to be taken alive. This Roman centurion disobeyed those orders.**

No Mercy

King Henry II of England (1133–1189) thought he would get a compliant head of the Church when he made his bosom buddy, Thomas Becket, Archbishop of Canterbury in 1161. The two had a history of making merry and enjoying each other's company. As Lord Chancellor, Becket had supported the king in all his disputes with the Church. So keen was Henry to promote Becket that he had him ordained as a priest, then a bishop, and finally the archbishop, in only a few days.

However, once he was placed in the holy office, Becket donned a symbolic and literal "hair shirt" and became a fierce advocate of the Catholic Church. In common with other European kings at the time, Henry was seeking to limit the power and wealth of the Church. Priests could commit even the worst crimes, such as murder, rape, and sodomy, but be tried in an ecclesiastical court, which almost invariably let them off. Henry sought to bring priests into the criminal law courts, but Becket fought him tooth and nail. To make matters worse, Becket used his powers to excommunicate other bishops appointed by the king. The relationship between the two men deteriorated until finally the frustrated king called out in his royal court, "Who will rid me of this meddlesome priest?"

Whether this was a genuine demand for Becket to be assassinated or words spoken in anger, four knights decided to curry favor and traveled to Canterbury to kill the archbishop, arriving on December 29, 1170. Hugh de Morville, William de Tracy, Richard le Breton, and Reginald FitzUrse covered their mail and swords with robes and confronted Becket during vespers, demanding that he absolve the excommunicated bishops. He refused, and the knights set upon him. As they attempted to drag him out of the cathedral, the prelate hung on to one of the columns, enraging the knights further.

LEFT **Henry II, who may have ordered the assassination of Archbishop Thomas Becket.**

While one sought to hold monks and parishioners at bay, FitzUrse lunged at Becket, shearing off the crown of his head. The prelate stumbled and knelt on the floor near a door to the monastic cloister. He called for mercy but was given none as another blow landed on his head. A monk called Edward Grim almost had his arm severed as he tried to protect the archbishop, but survived to tell the tale of the assassination. A third blow brought Becket down on all fours. Wounded, with blood streaming down his face, Becket moaned that he was ready to "embrace death" and was duly obliged when the third knight struck him a blow that split his skull in two with such force that the sword blade shattered against the cathedral's stone floor.

ABOVE **Four knights descended on Becket in Canterbury Cathedral. All witnesses agree that the knights' repeated blows spread his brains over the cathedral floor.**

The final act in the carnage occurred when one of the knights pinned Becket's bruised and bloodied neck to the floor with one foot and stamped down on his ruined head until it was reduced to skull and brain mincemeat. The knights fled. Far from being rewarded by a grateful king, they were excommunicated by the pope and banished to the Holy Land to do penance.

When Becket's body was being prepared for burial, his hair shirt was removed and found to be crawling with so many lice that they seemed to flow over his ruined back like "a wave."

Henry received no comfort from the killing. Pressure built upon him to such an extent that four years later, he felt compelled to walk to Canterbury barefoot, beg his old friend's forgiveness at his tomb, and be lashed by 80 monks wielding birch rods.

HE CALLED FOR MERCY BUT WAS GIVEN NONE AS ANOTHER BLOW LANDED ON HIS HEAD. A MONK CALLED EDWARD GRIM ALMOST HAD HIS ARM SEVERED AS HE TRIED TO PROTECT THE ARCHBISHOP, BUT SURVIVED TO TELL THE TALE OF THE ASSASSINATION.

The Last Bath

The French Revolution began in 1789 with the ideals of creating a new society based on equality, justice, and freedom. It soon degenerated into a frenzied bloodbath as the new rulers sought to eliminate entire classes of society. The guillotine was the weapon of choice, and other revolutionaries, such as Lenin and Mao Tse Tung, were to follow in the footsteps of these first bloody revolutionaries.

One man who was largely responsible for the bloodletting of the French experiment was undoubtedly Jean Paul Marat. "Man has the right to deal with his oppressors by devouring their palpitating hearts." It was with words such as these that Marat, through his rabidly fanatic newspaper "The Friend of The People," incited more and more desperate revolutionary bloodletting. He was held partially responsible for the September massacres in 1792, in which the Parisian mob, egged on by Marat and his like, cleared the prisons of class enemies. At one institution, 378 prisoners were hacked into pieces and piled in heaps. Carts were loaded with the mangled remains by women who pinned ears to their dresses as souvenirs. Sometimes the dismembered carcasses of priests and nobles were used as tables and chairs by the "Septembriseurs" (as the assassins were known) as they refreshed themselves with good red wine and bread before resuming their labors. Marie Gredeler, a woman with links to the royal court, had her breasts cut off, her feet nailed to the ground, and a bonfire lit beneath her spread-eagled legs. Princesse de Lamballe, Marie Antoinette's closest friend, was stripped and raped before her breasts were cut off. One of the young lady's legs was fired out of a cannon, her heart was eaten, and her genitals were removed and impaled, along with her pretty head, on top of some pikes.

LEFT **Marat's fiery oratory and poison pen contributed to one of the first outbreaks of class warfare. He was determined to destroy the old ruling classes.**

ABOVE Marat was seen as the champion of the "*sans-culottes*"—those without trousers. His relentless revolutionary activity had had an effect on his health.

But this was not enough for Marat. In September 1792, he was elected to the National Convention (the revolutionary parliament) and became an architect of "the Terror," drawing up long lists of those he felt threatened the revolution. His many years in hiding had allowed him to build up a network of spies, which he used to accuse others of opposing the revolution.

The sickness within Marat's soul was mirrored in his diseased and putrid body. Although originally trained as doctor, he had contracted a multiplicity of skin complaints. It is possible he suffered from Dermatitis herpetiformis, an extremely unpleasant rash that leads to pus-filled blisters forming all over the body, uncontrollable itching, and infection. This is now associated with gluten intolerance. Alternatively, he may have suffered from phototoxic dermatitis caused by an allergic reaction to sunlight. Whatever the complaint, it meant that for the last years of his life the rabid revolutionary was mostly confined to a large, copper-lined tub where he soaked in various concoctions, including oatmeal, to try to ease the desperate itching caused by his condition.

It was in this rancid tub that Charlotte Corday found the tyrant on July 13, 1793. She was a member of the moderate "Girondin" party who was outraged at the treatment of her fellows by Jacobins such as Marat. She managed to wheedle her way into

ABOVE **Charlotte Corday gained access to Marat's chamber with a list of potential new victims. She used the opportunity to strike a blow for human rights.**

Marat's presence by claiming she had a list of counterrevolutionaries who he could add to his death list. This cheered Marat immensely, and he chuckled and drooled over the list, declaring that all who went against the revolution would be rounded up and guillotined the very next day.

At this, Corday whipped a large butcher's knife from her dress and leapt upon Marat, stabbing him multiple times as she towered over the emaciated politician. He was, according to all reports, near death anyway, and could not put up much of a struggle. Her blade punctured his lung and slashed his windpipe. Marat must have gasped for air in the last moments of his life, desperately trying to survive the mortal wounds inflicted upon his already-ravaged body. The artist Jacques-Louis David portrays Marat as dying in almost blissful peace. Marat's death mask portrays a different story, showing the dying Jacobin's contorted and agonized features. And David's portrait is unrealistic in another respect. It portrays Corday's knife on the floor, whereas she left it sticking out of his chest when she was wrestled to the floor and captured by Marat's porter.

On July 17, 1793, Corday was beheaded, but not before she had impressed all with her courage in the days leading up to the trial and execution. She was described as serene and beautiful to the end.

HE WAS, ACCORDING TO ALL REPORTS, NEAR DEATH ANYWAY AND COULD NOT PUT UP MUCH OF A STRUGGLE. HER BLADE PUNCTURED HIS LUNG AND SLASHED HIS WINDPIPE. MARAT MUST HAVE GASPED FOR AIR IN THE LAST MOMENTS OF HIS LIFE, DESPERATELY TRYING TO SURVIVE THE MORTAL WOUNDS INFLICTED UPON HIS ALREADY-RAVAGED BODY.

The Red Martyr

Rosa Luxemburg and her companion had the misfortune to initiate a Communist revolt just as the right-wing nationalist Freikorps were regaining control in postwar Germany.

Rosa was born on March 5, 1871, in what is now Poland. She helped found the Polish Social Democratic Party and the Spartacus League, which then became the Communist Party of Germany. She moved to Germany in 1898 and settled in Berlin. While many other Communists believed in a gradual move towards communism through democratic means, she believed in violent revolution. The problem for Rosa was that she was not as violent as the paramilitary Freikorps.

At the outbreak of World War I, she went into alliance with Karl Liebknecht and founded the Spartakusbund, or Spartacus League. This party of radical leftists was determined to end the war and establish a proletarian government. They were arrested and imprisoned for their antiwar sentiments.

With the signing of the armistice in November 1918, the two were released and immediately began preparing for an armed takeover. This led to a number of armed clashes in Berlin, and she earned the epithet "Bloody Rosa." In December 1918, they became founders of the German Communist Party. Throughout the industrial centers of Germany, Communists raised the red flag of revolt and sought to begin a revolution just as had happened in Russia in 1917. It was called the Spartacist Revolt.

BELOW **Rosa Luxemburg was a radical communist agitator who wanted Germany to become a Bolshevik state like Lenin's Russia.**

With their revolutionary ardor fanned by newspapers such as *Die Rote Fahne* (The Red Flag), workers, sailors, and soldiers started massed strikes and demonstrations, while revolutionary councils seized town halls, barracks, and armories throughout the western and central regions of Germany. Opposition newspapers were closed down and banks seized. Red machine-gun crews and snipers took up positions in the center of many towns, ready to defend their new soviets.

Class warfare was on the agenda, and a "Red Terror" began as political opponents were rounded up and executed. Officers who tried to bring sailors back to duty in the massive naval base at Kiel were shot out of hand by their crew and tossed overboard. In the Ruhr town of Bottrop, the "Red Army" captured 40 raw soldiers and bludgeoned them to death with clubs. Mobs surrounded columns of soldiers and police and beat the officers to death before throwing them into rivers.

While the army (Reichswehr) was seen as unreliable by the new government, extreme right-wing paramilitary groups called Freikorps were established and it was their job to destroy the nascent Red republics. Mainly composed of ex-soldiers who had been brutalized at the front, they were often led by fanatical officers determined that Germany should regain her former military glory. Many of the Freikorps were brigade strength, with up to 5,000 men complete with artillery, armor, and even air force assets. Their superior discipline and training allowed them to overcome the Red militias.

Using the right-wing media to exaggerate Communist atrocities, the White Terror far eclipsed the Red Terror as the Freikorps regained control of Germany for the new government. Moving against the Spartacist Uprising in Berlin in January 1919, precedents for later brutality were established. Operating against the revolutionary headquarters in East Berlin, tanks and artillery were used to bombard the enemy positions before they were stormed. The Spartacist defenders had to fight to the finish, as any who tried to surrender were butchered on the spot. Elevators and stairwells were no refuge, as the Freikorps troops bludgeoned or shot prisoners. Resistance was ruthlessly suppressed, and only the occasional rooftop sniper (nicknamed *Dachkaninchen*, or roof rabbits) continued to resist.

After several days in hiding, the Spartacist leaders, Karl Liebknecht and Rosa Luxemburg, were arrested on January 15, 1919, by government authorities. Taken to the Hotel Eden, both were ruthlessly beaten, knocked down, and dragged

LEFT This KPD (Communist Party of Germany) poster calls for a workers' uprising. The right-wing Freikorps smashed the revolt with brute force.

around. Taken one at a time out of a side entrance, they encountered Otto Runge, who beat them with his rifle butt before both were put into separate cars and taken to a park. Told that they had to get out of the cars due to a flat tire, both were shot while "attempting to escape." Several weeks later, Rosa's battered corpse was fished out of the Landwehr Canal.

ABOVE **Street battles erupted in the major German cities. Large amounts of heavy weaponry left over from World War I were used by both sides.**

Luxemburg became the first German Communist leader to be murdered. The Red rebellion was snuffed out over several years of brutality. Adolf Hitler witnessed the street warfare and learned his lessons well. He adapted the techniques of the Freikorps, and thousands of other Communist leaders would die in street brawls and concentration camps during the 1930s and 40s.

Ice Ax in Exile

Lenin was the master of terror. Trotsky and Stalin were his apprentices. All three were ruthless men and responsible for millions of deaths. In the power struggle that developed after Lenin's death, Stalin came out on top. Unable to kill the popular hero of the Red Army, he allowed Trotsky to flee into exile. Trotsky remained a thorn in Stalin's side, and the dictator determined to kill him as soon as he could. Bombs and bullets didn't work. An ice ax did.

Lev Davidovich Bronstein was born of Jewish parents in the Ukraine in 1879, and he soon became a fanatical Marxist agitator. Exiled to Siberia, he took the name "Trotsky" from the head jailer in his Siberian prison. Escaping in 1902, he was in St.

ABOVE Leon Trotsky orchestrated the Bolshevik takeover of St. Petersburg in 1917. His charismatic leadership allowed Lenin's party to win the civil war that followed.

BELOW Bolshevik control of the railways combined with Trotsky's ruthless discipline allowed the Red Army to destroy the White Army.

Petersburg in time to set up the first Soviet (Workers' and Soldiers' Council) during the 1905 Revolution sparked by Bloody Sunday, when hundreds of demonstrators were killed or wounded.

Falling under Lenin's spell, he joined the Bolsheviks in July 1917 and turned his skills to ensuring that the October Revolution was a success. Trotsky proved to be a logistical genius. He organized the Red Guard from a disparate collection of Lithuanian soldiers and undisciplined workers and established the blueprint for a successful revolution. On October 18, the Red Guard swung into action and seized vital infrastructure in St. Petersburg, including rail and river crossings, as well as the Winter Palace, seat of the Provisional Government.

As the civil war spread throughout Russia, it was Trotsky in his armored train who could be found wherever the fighting was hottest. Carrying printing presses for propaganda purposes and accompanied by a crack team of Chekists (secret police), wherever Trotsky appeared, the front stabilized, and the White Army was forced to retreat.

Trotsky had a simple rule to ensure his army kept fighting. He issued a decree: "Any soldier who deserts will be shot. Any soldier who sells his weapon will be shot. Any soldier who fraternizes with the enemy will be shot."

Trotsky was not much of a people person and had a reputation for rudeness and arrogance. He was not much of a politician

either, and Stalin was able to gather his many enemies and ensure that his rival was exiled from Moscow. At Lenin's funeral in 1924, which Trotsky did not attend, Stalin declared himself Lenin's successor. He expelled Trotsky from the Communist Party in 1927, exiled him to the wilds of Central Asia in 1928, and expelled him from Soviet Russia in 1929.

Trotsky fled through several countries before ending up in Mexico. In 1936, he was tried in absentia and declared a traitor. The exiled ideologue refused to be silenced and wrote books and pamphlets attacking Stalin. His sympathizers in Russia helped

Stalin's "Wet Work" Specialists

Stalin was no stranger to assassination. He had a branch within the NKVD whose specialty was "wet work" in foreign countries. The NKVD—the People's Commissariat for Internal Affairs—had replaced the Cheka as the Bolshevik secret police.

The "NKVD Foreign Section" was largely concerned with running operatives in hostile Western nations who specialized in observation, infiltration, espionage, fifth columnist recruitment, and intelligence gathering. Within the Foreign Section was the harmless-sounding "Administration for Special Tasks." Their activities were anything but harmless, and this organization, based in Paris, concentrated on assassination and kidnapping of ideological enemies. By 1938 the division had 212 trained killers operating throughout Europe. These ruthless spies were trained in a range of assassination techniques, including poisons and bombs. Many defecting Soviets or ex-White generals were kidnapped or killed, and the most famous victim of the Administration for Special Tasks was Leon Trotsky.

ABOVE **Joseph Stalin took power after Lenin's premature death. He dealt ruthlessly with his opponents and destroyed countless individuals and whole communities.**

ABOVE **Leon Trotsky depicted in Diego Rivera's fresco *Man at the Crossroads*. Even though many see him as a hero, he was always a difficult character.**

to spread these pamphlets, and Stalin decided he had to take action.

Trotsky found it difficult to get along with anyone. Initially, he lived in Mexico with the famed artist Diego Rivera, but the argumentative Bolshevik soon got his marching orders and moved out into his own home.

Meanwhile, Stalin began his campaign of murder. In 1938, members of an NKVD "wet team" (see feature box on page 117) gained entrance to a Paris hospital where Trotsky's son was a patient. Using subterfuge and bribery, they turned a routine operation into a botched deadly appendectomy. The team then beheaded Trotsky's Paris secretary.

Then, on May 24, 1940, 21 men dressed as Mexican police burst into Trotsky's house in Mexico City. They threw lit sticks of dynamite around before bursting into his bedroom and spraying 300 bullets. After the dust had settled, Trotsky and his wife emerged from under the bed where they had taken shelter. Miraculously, the couple were unharmed but the assassins took off with one of the guards, a New Yorker named Robert Sheldon, whose decomposing body was found several weeks later in a deserted house nearby.

Whatever his failings, Trotsky was no idiot. He turned his house into a veritable fortress. Towering 15-foot (4.5-meter) brick walls circled the building, broken only by three machine-gun-armed pillboxes. Steel gates were installed, and his supporters paid for a small army of bodyguards.

Trotsky protected himself from his enemies, but not his friends. A charming young Canadian called Frank Jackson was introduced to Trotsky's inner circle. He was a keen listener and flattered Trotsky whenever he was invited around for dinner at the revolutionary exile's compound. It is a remarkable fact that no one ever sought to find out what Jackson did for a living or where he acquired his almost inexhaustible supply of funds. Trotsky had a hatred for Bourgeoisie flatterers, but he accepted this young man at face value.

In fact, had Trotsky looked a little deeper he would have discovered that Frank Jackson was a Soviet-trained assassin and saboteur named Jaime Ramón Mercader. A fanatical Stalinist, he was convinced by his mother to wheedle his way into the exile's confidence so that he could do away with him. His mother, Caridad Mercader, had already been awarded the Order of Lenin for doing Stalin's bidding and knocking off some of the dictator's enemies.

When he wasn't supping at the Russian's table, Jackson loved climbing nearby mountains and developed a proficiency with an ice ax. In August 1940, he put his skills to deadly use.

At 5:30 in the early evening of August 20, Jackson arrived at Trotsky's fortress. So trusted was the young man that he knew he wouldn't be searched. He had armed himself with a revolver, a dagger, and an ice ax under his spacious coat. The assassin obviously had the run of the place and made his way to the study, where he secreted the ice ax in an accessible location. He then joined Trotsky in the yard and asked him to look over an article he had written. If there was something Trotsky loved above all else, it was giving his opinion, and he readily agreed to help. The two men moved into the study in earnest discussion.

Mercader/Jackson made his move. Within a few minutes, raised voices were heard from the study. The assassin had retrieved the ax, turned to Trotsky, and, closing his eyes, sunk the ax spike deep into the Bolshevik's brain. Trotsky gave an unearthly wailing shriek—many who heard it could never forget the piercing sound. But Trotsky would not go easily, and he turned on the assassin and tried to barge past him and escape. Mercator pulled out his pistol to fire into his victim's back, but before he could do so, two bodyguards burst into the room, chopped the gun out of his

BELOW **Ramón Mercader was badly beaten by Trotsky's bodyguards and barely survived to stand trial.**

hand, and began to pummel him to within an inch of his life. It was Trotsky who saved the young man. He told the guards to lay off as, in his words, "He has a story to tell."

The plan had misfired. Caridad was waiting outside the house in a getaway car ready to drive her son to safety when he snuck out after doing the deed. Trotsky's resistance had scotched that plan.

Trotsky had blood pouring out of the wound in his head, and he collapsed on the dining room floor. While his wife cradled the head of her injured husband, an ambulance was called. Both victim and assassin were rushed to Mexico City Hospital, where they were placed in wards on the same floor. Trotsky died at 7.25 p.m. on August 21, 26 hours after the attack. He was lucid for much of the time, but blood loss and brain damage finished him off. Mercader recovered from his beating almost immediately.

The assassin was sentenced to 20 years' imprisonment in 1943, although he was released in 1960 before being deported to Communist Czechoslovakia.

Malcolm X Sought Peace Too Late

He was born as Malcolm Little on May 19, 1925, in Omaha, Nebraska. From an early age, he experienced the worst that racist America could throw at him and his family. However, it was black rivals who killed him with a shotgun blast to the belly on February 21, 1965.

Born to a Baptist minister, his family was regularly set upon by white supremacists. His maternal grandmother had been raped by a red-haired white man, and this genetic trait was carried through to Malcolm Little. The family home was torched when he was four years old, and it seems that in 1931 his father was beaten, thrown under a street car, and nearly cut in half before he died. This left a burning anger in the young man, and after dropping out of school he shifted around before settling in New York, where he embarked on a career of petty theft, drug dealing, and pimping. In 1946 he was arrested and sentenced to ten years' prison.

LEFT **This photograph was taken about a year before Malcolm X's assassination. His fiery oratory alienated many powerful organizations.**

Bizarre Assassins' Weapons

THE PEN IS MIGHTIER THAN THE SWORD, so the famous saying goes. The earliest pen guns were invented in the 1920s and soon became popular with intelligence agencies. The first mass-produced pen gun was the "Stinger" used by the OSS (Office of Strategic Services, forerunner of the CIA) during World War II. A single shot .22, it was small enough to be concealed anywhere on the body or even in a packet of cigarettes. It had a rounded end so it could be concealed in bodily cavities. In 2011, a North Korean Special Forces operative was arrested with poison pens in his possession. One had a hypodermic apparatus that was intended to poison Park Sang-hak, a North Korean defector, while the other was armed with a poison-filled bullet.

The cyanide gun was undoubtedly one of the most efficient guns in the KGB arsenal. The ungainly looking weapon first crushed a cyanide capsule before an aerosol sprayed the lethal fumes over the target's face. Cyanide can be absorbed through the skin and leads to symptoms exactly like a heart attack. The KGB agent Bohdan Stashynsky was the best-known practitioner with this weapon and killed at least two Ukrainian dissidents. He would lie in wait with the gun wrapped in a newspaper before whipping it out and spraying them. Even a small dose was lethal, necessitating that Stashynsky take an antidote prior to its use.

Built in Britain during World War II, the Welrod (pictured) was disguised to look like a bicycle pump but, once assembled, became one of the deadliest assassin's weapons of all time. Thousands were made and supplied to resistance groups in World War II, although many found their way into the hands of the IRA. Its handle was an eight-shot magazine with a simple bolt action to the rear of the handle, though usually just the one 9mm fragmentation bullet did the job. The barrel was designed to slow down the bullet and retard the gases from the cartridge's discharge, reducing the amount of noise. The entire barrel was a long suppressor (silencer) and it was designed to be fired at point-blank range into the intended target so that their body would also act as an extra noise suppressor.

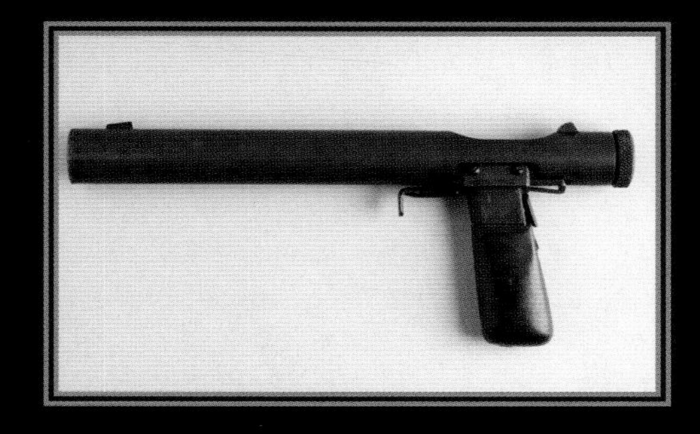

ABOVE Muhammad Ali listens to Elijah Muhammad speak to followers of the Nation of Islam in 1964.

This was a turning point in the young man's life. He began to educate himself and fell in with the radical Elijah Muhammad's Black Muslim organization. This sect had some pretty far-fetched ideas and believed that all races were in fact black but had been "bleached" by a mad scientist called Yakub. More logical, though, was the cult's practice of changing their names from what their slave-owning heritage had bestowed upon them. Malcolm Little became Malcolm X. He also gave up alcohol, tobacco, and pre-marital sex (he married in 1958 and had six children).

In the 1950s and 60s, the civil rights movement grew, and while moderates followed Martin Luther King, more militant blacks followed organizations such as Elijah Muhammad's renamed Nation of Islam.

Malcolm X became the chief spokesman for the Nation of Islam. His speeches dripped with hatred for whites. When a plane carrying 120 white Americans crashed in France, killing all of them, he welcomed it as a gift from god. Even when JFK, a strong supporter of civil rights, was killed in 1963, Malcolm offended nearly every American by tacitly supporting the assassination. This was too much for Elijah Muhammad, who moved to expel the radical firebrand from his movement. Undaunted, Malcolm X stepped up his vitriolic speeches.

That is, until 1964, when he visited Mecca. Soon after his return, he penned the "Letter from Mecca." This revealed a new, sensitive Malcolm X, who was determined to work with the establishment "through ballots not bullets" to achieve racial harmony and equality. He even sent out peace feelers to the camp of Martin Luther King.

However, this epiphany set Malcolm X on a collision course with both his old comrades from Nation of Islam and his more recently enrolled fanatical followers. One or both organizations were out to get him. The family's home was firebombed, and he, his wife, and their daughters had a narrow escape from the flames. No organization took responsibility, although the Nation of Islam seemed the most likely suspects. Soon afterward, a group of three men were chased away from the family's temporary residence at the New York Hilton. They had enquired from the bellhop where their room was, but security was alerted, and the three took off.

The following day, February 21, 1965, Malcolm X, surrounded by his bodyguards, made his way to the Audubon Ballroom in Harlem, where he was scheduled to address 400 followers. He rose to the lectern, and his bodyguards arrayed themselves between him and the audience.

Just as the civil rights activist began his speech, a loud scuffle broke out. Two men began to fight each other, one accusing the other of trying to pick his pockets. Malcom enjoined them "Now, Brothers, be cool," and four of his bodyguards moved to sort out the disturbance.

At the same time, a small fire broke out at the rear of the congregation. The distracted guards were torn between the two situations. Seizing his chance, 22-year-old Talmadge Hayer of Paterson, New Jersey, ran up the center aisle, pulled out a shotgun, and discharged both barrels through the lectern straight into Malcom's chest. Wood

BELOW **New York's finest rush the wounded Malcolm X to hospital. All to no avail—14 bullet wounds ended the activist's life.**

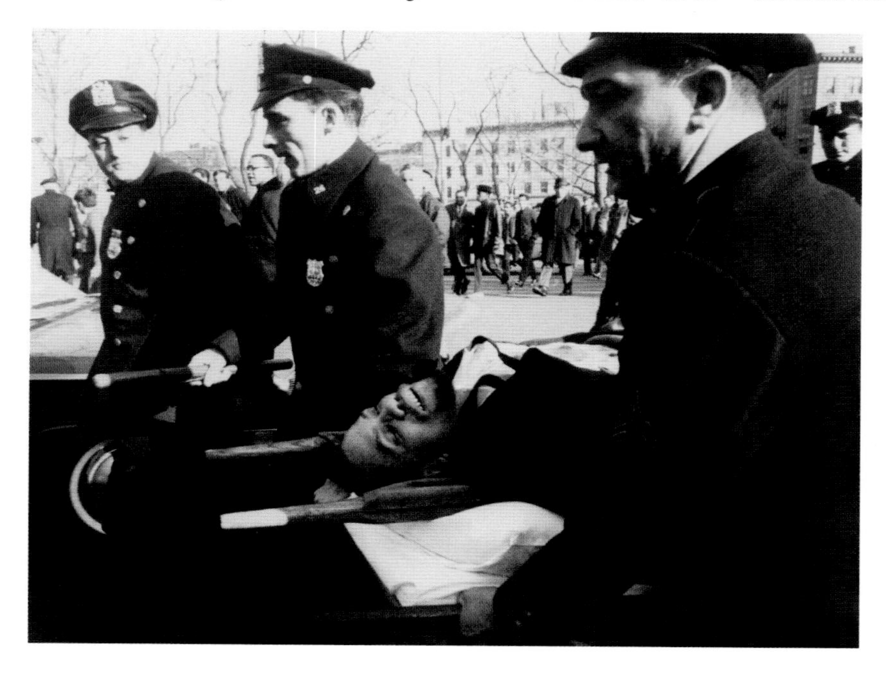

ABOVE **Bullet holes peppered the back of the stage where Malcom X was shot on February 21, 1965.**

fragments and lead shot ripped through his torso. The two who had instigated the first distraction leapt on to the stage, pulled out pistols, and emptied their bullets into X's prostrate body.

The three attackers bolted through different doors but Hayer was winged by one of the bodyguard's bullets before being set upon by the enraged crowd. He only just survived when arriving police pulled them off him.

The mortally wounded activist was rushed to nearby Columbia Presbyterian Medical Center. Placed on a gurney, doctors frantically tried to keep him alive but he died soon after arrival. Fit and healthy at 38, not even he could survive 14 bullet wounds.

A counterattack was launched by Malcom X's supporters. Mosques connected to Nation of Islam were firebombed, and the darkest threats were issued against Elijah Muhammad. Two more hard men from that organization were accused and jailed for the crime. As the years went by, it emerged that the higher echelons of Nation of Islam were responsible for planning the attack and carrying it out.

Twenty thousand people filed past Malcolm X's body as it was displayed in a glass-topped casket in a Harlem funeral home, and 1,500 attended his funeral.

Malcolm X allowed black Americans to embrace their heritage and find pride in the tribulations of the past. Many activist groups were founded in his shadow, and he is now seen as one of the most influential African Americans of the 20th century.

Going Up to the Mountain

Martin Luther King was born in 1929 in Atlanta, Georgia. Emerging as the leader of the civil rights movement in the USA, he tried to use his talent for speaking to gain rights for his people. His enemies were prepared to use violence.

Racing through school, King was a talented youngster who could recite whole tracts of the Bible and sing lengthy hymns as early as five years old. As an activist, he scored his first victory against racism as the head of the Dexter Avenue Baptist Church in Montgomery, Alabama. His stirring rhetoric and rich and resonant baritone led the campaign, starting in December 1955, to boycott segregated city buses in the Southern town. It was his first victory, and in November 1956 the US Supreme Court vetoed the Alabama laws that legalized segregated buses. White supremacists had their target, and violence would pursue King until the end of his days. They would stop at nothing, and in early 1956, soon after the bus boycott began, his family home was all but destroyed with a massive bomb blast. Fortunately, the Kings were not at home. It was the opening shot in the campaign of violence against King.

Martin Luther King believed in peaceful protest, much as Mahatma Gandhi had practiced. This was not reciprocated by Southern authorities. Police, militia, and the National Guard were often deployed to continue the human rights abuses heaped upon the African American. But King had a more lethal enemy: J. Edgar Hoover, the head of the FBI. Hoover saw King's quest for human rights as un-American.

In January 1957, King and 115 other black leaders formed the "Southern Christian Leadership Conference." The protest movement spread, not so much because of the rightness of their cause or the fiery preaching of King and his supporters, but mainly because of the ham-fisted attempts to close his movement down. Nothing demonstrated this better than the 1963 nonviolent march through Birmingham, Alabama. Although King was arrested and

RIGHT **Dr. Martin Luther King called for the non-violent overthrow of entrenched racism in America during the 1950s and 60s.**

locked in the local slammer, his grass roots support ensured that thousands of young black activists, many of them schoolchildren, were determined to march against segregation. Setting off from various locations, their peaceful march was intercepted by the local police, who used savage attack dogs to maul marchers and aimed fire hoses that could "peel the bark right-offa tree" with their pressure at the marchers.

The press leapt upon the story. Businesses in Birmingham were boycotted, and photographs of innocents being attacked and beaten were plastered across every newspaper. Even the Kennedys got involved, and the First Lady, Jacqueline Kennedy, communicated with King while he was imprisoned. When he was finally released, the Kings left town, and two hours later their motel room was blown to smithereens, as was his brother's house. When the police arrived to investigate, thousands of blacks began rioting. Vehicles and houses were torched, and stabbings and beatings were common. Three thousand federal troops were needed to restore order. But King won. From June 1963, the Jim Crow signs were removed, and segregation was no more.

Following on from this successful campaign, King attained a national profile. In August 1963, he gave his famous "I Have a Dream" speech before 250,000 followers. By the end of 1964, Congress had passed the Civil Rights Act, and King had earned the Nobel Peace Prize. Nevertheless, the fight went on—it was one

BELOW **Martin Luther King giving the famous "I Have a Dream" speech on August 28, 1963, at the Lincoln Memorial, Washington, DC.**

thing for the politicians in Washington to legislate equal rights, but quite another to get people to change their ways. In 1965, at Selma, Alabama, 600 protesters marched for voting rights and were mercilessly beaten by state troopers. Many were hospitalized and several killed. King whipped up support for another march, and in what could be seen as his second great victory, the Federal Voting Rights Act became law.

ABOVE **J. Edgar Hoover, head of the FBI. No African Americans were allowed to be agents in his organization.**

King then broadened his perspective and began to protest against poverty within the USA, as well as American involvement in the Vietnam War. This earned the enmity of J. Edgar Hoover. The FBI was itself something of a segregationist organization at the time, as there were no African American agents within the bureau. Hoover established an entire task force to discredit King and the organizations he belonged to. Infiltrators joined these organizations and phone tapping was used in a desperate effort to blacken the reputation of King and his followers. Anonymous cartoons and vicious tracts were issued in a remorseless anti-King campaign as Hoover sought to "remove King from the national scene." It is possible that the FBI facilitated King's assassination; they certainly squibbed the investigation.

Violence continued to follow King's peaceful demonstrations. On March 28, 1968, he led a protest in Memphis, Tennessee, to support a strike of 1,300 sanitation workers. Once again, the police attacked the march. One 16-year-old was killed, 62 were injured, and 200 were arrested on what was dubbed by the outraged press "Bloody Sunday." King himself was targeted by anonymous death threats, and the plane that was scheduled to fly him on his return to Memphis on April 3 was delayed at Atlanta airport due to a report that there was a bomb planted on board. At Memphis that night, he addressed a rally of 2,000 supporters and seemed to almost acquiesce to an early death, saying he had already gone "up to the mountain."

After this rally, an exhausted King checked into room 305 of the Lorraine Motel in Memphis. He rose late and then had a conference with some aides in room 306. At

ABOVE Immediately after the shooting, many witnesses were able to point at the source of the gunfire. King is mortally wounded, lying at their feet.

6 p.m., King emerged from room 306 in a black suit and leaned over the railing of the motel balcony to speak with Jesse Jackson, who was standing in the parking lot below. King chatted with his friends, discussing music and clothes, cheerfully biding his time until they had to leave for another rally.

Suddenly, a mighty crack was heard. King grabbed at his throat and sank to the floor of the concrete balcony. Blood poured from a gaping wound in his neck—a bullet had ripped into his throat and blown off his tie. Police who had been stationed at the motel to protect King swarmed around to the rear. King had been on the balcony for three minutes, and in that unguarded moment his fate was sealed.

King's aides ran to him. One pressed a towel to his throat to try to stem the blood loss while another spread a blanket to try to stop him going into cardiac shock. The bullet had exploded through the right side of King's neck and jaw, resulting in a fleshy wound 3 inches (7.6 centimeters) long and 2 inches (5 centimeters) wide. His spinal cord was severed and his neck vertebrae were shattered. Even if he had survived, King would have been a quadriplegic.

It was not only the police who made a mess of the situation. It took an ambulance ten minutes to arrive and collect the mortally wounded King. Arriving at St Joseph's Hospital, surgeons frantically tried to save him, but at 7:05 p.m., life signs terminated and King was no more.

This was too much for generations of oppressed African Americans. Ignoring King's message of peaceful protest, blacks poured on to the streets throughout America, and violent riots erupted throughout the country. Black sections of the major cities such as Detroit, Boston, Chicago, Washington, DC, and New York saw buildings trashed, stores looted, and cars burned. In some towns, business came to halt for up to two days as office workers fled home to escape the violent protests. In Chicago alone, 6,000 National Guard troops were called up to stem the violence. Seven were killed and hundreds arrested. In Washington, DC, more than 3,000 arrests were made, eight blacks were killed, 620 fires had been lit, and 705 people were injured, including policemen, firemen, and soldiers. A division of troops was called in to patrol the streets and restore order. Things slowly calmed down, with King's widow, Coretta Scott King, pleading for calm and nonviolent protests.

Who had killed King? A white Southern lowlife who plumbed the depths of society, just as King soared the highest peaks of oratory, had killed the Civil Rights leader. James Earl Ray had purchased a cheap used rifle and with a single bullet assassinated one of the most

BELOW **Widespread rioting followed the assassination as African Americans vented their rage. Even in the heart of Washington, DC, some buildings were destroyed.**

significant Americans ever born. Ray was born into poverty in Alton, Illinois, in 1928 and began a career as a petty criminal. Sentenced to 20 years' imprisonment in 1960 for armed hold-ups, he escaped in 1967 and became a wandering drifter. He took odd jobs and had a reputation as a hard drinker. On April 1, Ray drove to Memphis in a white Mustang. He bought a Remington .30-06 pump-action hunting rifle with telescopic sight and checked into a local rooming house situated behind the Lorraine Motel. Late in the afternoon of August 4, Ray positioned himself in the upstairs

BELOW **James Earl Ray had a long criminal history. These mug shots date back to 1952. It is still not clear why he shot King.**

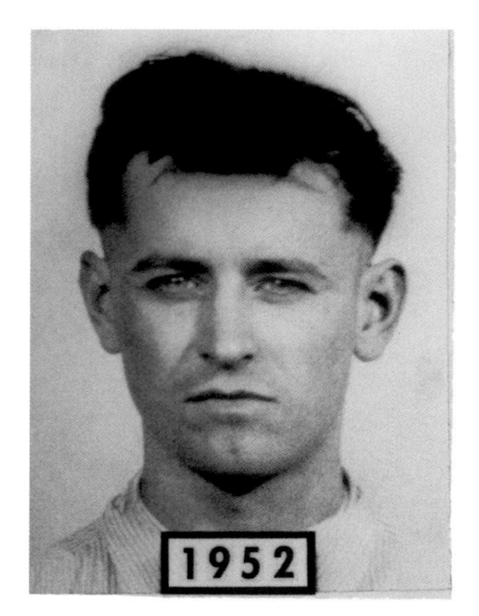

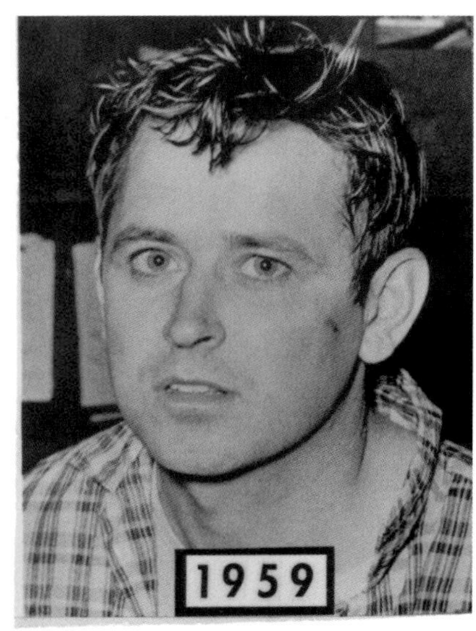

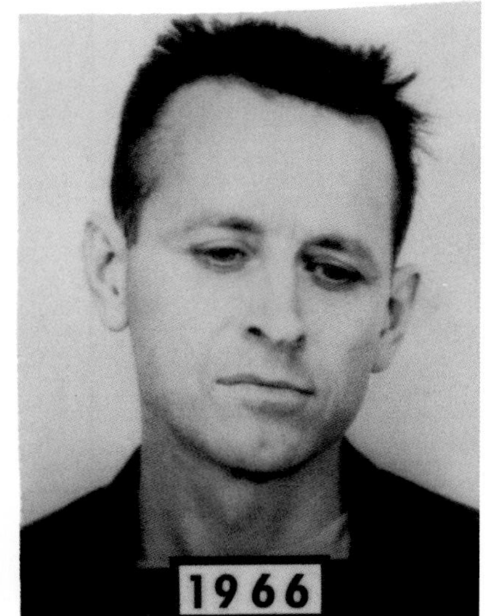

LATE IN THE AFTERNOON OF AUGUST 4, RAY POSITIONED HIMSELF IN THE UPSTAIRS COMMUNAL BATHROOM AND DREW A BEAD ON THE BALCONY FRONTING THE ROOMS WHERE KING WAS STAYING.

communal bathroom and drew a bead on the balcony fronting the rooms where King was staying. To get the best shot, he had to stand in the bath with the rifle resting on the windowsill.

King emerged and was shot once by Ray. The assassin then bundled his possessions into a neatly wrapped parcel, deposited it in the doorway of an amusement arcade near the rooming house, and did a runner. The bundle contained the gun along with bullets, shaving cream, binoculars, nail clippers, and a radio with Ray's name on it. His fingerprints were on every item. In his room, they found that a large dresser had been moved in front of the rear window and a seat placed behind it—a perfect sniper's nest.

A keen-eyed witness had seen a white Mustang speed from the scene and had taken down the number. The FBI found that this was registered to the mysterious Eric Starvo Galt. They also traced the rifle to Birmingham, Alabama, where it had been sold to a man named Harvey Lowmyer—another of Ray's aliases.

A Remington .30-06 hunting rifle determined to be the murder weapon was found on a sidewalk about a block from the motel, almost directly in front of the rooming house registered to Galt. Upon entering, the Memphis police discovered Ray's setup, confirming this was indeed the sniper's room.

Mr. Ray spent several weeks in Toronto immediately after the assassination. Then he flew to London, to Portugal, and then back to London, where he was captured by Scotland Yard on June 8 as he was about to board a flight to Belgium. In his possession were two Canadian passports and a loaded gun.

Back in Memphis on March 10, 1969, his 41st birthday, Mr. Ray stood before Judge W. Preston Battle of Shelby County Criminal Court, pleaded guilty to the murder of Dr. King and was sentenced to 99 years' imprisonment, with no eligibility for parole before serving half that term. The plea, which waived his right to trial, enabled him to escape the electric chair.

After the sentence was passed down and the prospect of being electrocuted was no longer likely, Ray changed his story and claimed to be a patsy. Some doubts do remain, but the weight of evidence supports the idea that he was the lone assassin. The question of who funded his murderous activities and subsequent flight to London is still unanswered.

The assassin died of liver failure in April 1988 at the age of 70.

The Lethal Umbrella

Georgi Markov was the poster boy for the Bulgarian Communist Party Ministry of Culture. Despite coming from politically unreliable stock, his literary talents allowed him to rise within the Communist state and become an officially approved member of the Bulgarian Writers' Union. He obviously knew how to talk the talk and was given privileges that the average Bulgarian working stiff would have dreamed about. He was allowed to obtain a BMW and lived the high life in Sofia's artistic circles.

But Markov made the fatal mistake of biting the hand that fed him. In 1969, at the age of 40, he defected to London after visiting his brother in Italy.

Determined to rub salt into the wound, Markov became an announcer in the BBC World Service's Bulgarian Section as well as an anti-Communist spokesperson on the American-funded Radio Free Europe. An estimated five million Bulgarians tuned in to his cutting denunciations of the corrupt Communist system he had left behind. Todor Zhivkov, the Communist ruler of Bulgaria from 1971 to 1989, ordered that the signals be jammed. This didn't work, so he ordered the next best thing—assassination. Calling in specialist help from the KGB, Zhivkov demanded that Markov be silenced.

Markov was given several warnings via telephone calls to Radio Free Europe and his home. One caller made a stark threat—if he did not stop his new lectures, "Markov Speaks," he would be killed in such a cunning way that the authorities would believe he had simply died of natural causes. The continuing threats and resulting anxiety started to wear down the defector, and he said to his brother Georgi that he would almost welcome an early death! That death was soon to come, delivered by an umbrella.

On September 7, 1978, Markov was taking a well-deserved break from his double shift at the BBC by stretching his legs on Waterloo Bridge. He felt a sudden stinging pain in his thigh and turned around to see a heavy-set fellow with a wide-brimmed trilby bending over to retrieve his umbrella, which

LEFT **The fate of Bulgarian Defector Georgi Markov proved that escaping from behind the Iron Curtain was no guarantee of safety.**

Ricin

This nasty chemical is a naturally occurring element of the castor bean. Minute amounts can be lethal and ricin distilled from as few as eight beans is enough to kill a man. The symptoms of ricin poisoning aren't pleasant. The chemical compound stops cells from producing protein, leading to rapid cell death followed by major organ failure. The initial symptoms are violent vomiting, diarrhea, and stomach cramps. This is followed by hair loss, jaundice, severe dehydration, a collapse in blood pressure, and finally death.

RIGHT **Beans of the castor plant. This plant originated in Africa but is now widespread. One bean accidentally ingested can kill a child.**

he had apparently dropped by accident. Apologizing in a foreign accent, the man jumped into a taxi and sped off. Thinking no more of the incident, Markov went back to work.

Next morning, Markov was alarmed to find that the red bump on his leg had not gone down. He soon became feverish and then delirious. After three days of agonizing pain, the anti-Communist crusader died. His doctors had no idea what killed him.

During a police autopsy, the cause of death was established. The examining doctors found a tiny steel pellet in Markov's thigh, no larger than a pinhead. It had three small holes leading to a hollow center within which were found traces of the lethal poison ricin.

The KGB had loaded this deadly little missile into an umbrella fitted with a firing mechanism similar to that used in an air rifle and used it for this high-profile hit. The early warnings tipped off the British intelligence community, and if these had not occurred it is likely that there would not have been an autopsy.

It's likely that Zhivkov welcomed the publicity. He made no secret of his willingness to crack down on dissent, and it was this ruthless streak that allowed him to rule Bulgaria for his Russian masters for so long.

Death by Teapot

The leadership of Russia has also proved to be adept at assassination. Oligarchs, dissidents, and ex-spies who were opposed to the regime have suffered unpleasant deaths at the hands of assassins. No wonder, really. Putin and some of his closest supporters began their political careers as members of the KGB, Russia's secret service.

One assassination that could be at Putin's behest stands out. The ex-KGB agent Alexander Litvinenko was silenced using one of the most toxic substances known to man—polonium-210. This radioactive substance is not particularly dangerous when in a jar or bottle, and its nuclear rays cannot even pass through paper, let alone skin. But when polonium-210 is ingested, it is a radioactive time bomb. One thousandth of a milligram of the substance is enough to kill someone within a few weeks. One gram could kill an estimated 50 million people!

The unique agent decays into lead once within the body, and "alpha" radiation steals electrons from any molecule it encounters. This starts a chain reaction of destructive free radicals that damage cellular DNA and make cells commit suicide. Once it enters the bloodstream it attacks soft tissues throughout the body and especially targets the liver, kidneys, bone marrow, and spleen. Depending on the dose that is ingested, it can take minutes or days for the symptoms to appear. These include intense vomiting, diarrhea, hair loss, and lowered blood count.

Litvinenko allegedly earned Putin's dislike by filing reports stating that he was a pedophile and murderer, linked to the Mafia and Colombian drug barons. It seems that two KGB bodyguards, Andrei Lugovoy and Dmitry Kovtun, were dispatched to

A pot of tea was ordered. It came soon after—a white porcelain teapot filled with green tea, with lemon and honey on the side. It is possible that when Litvinenko wasn't watching, a dose of polonium-210 was added to the pot before he had his tea.

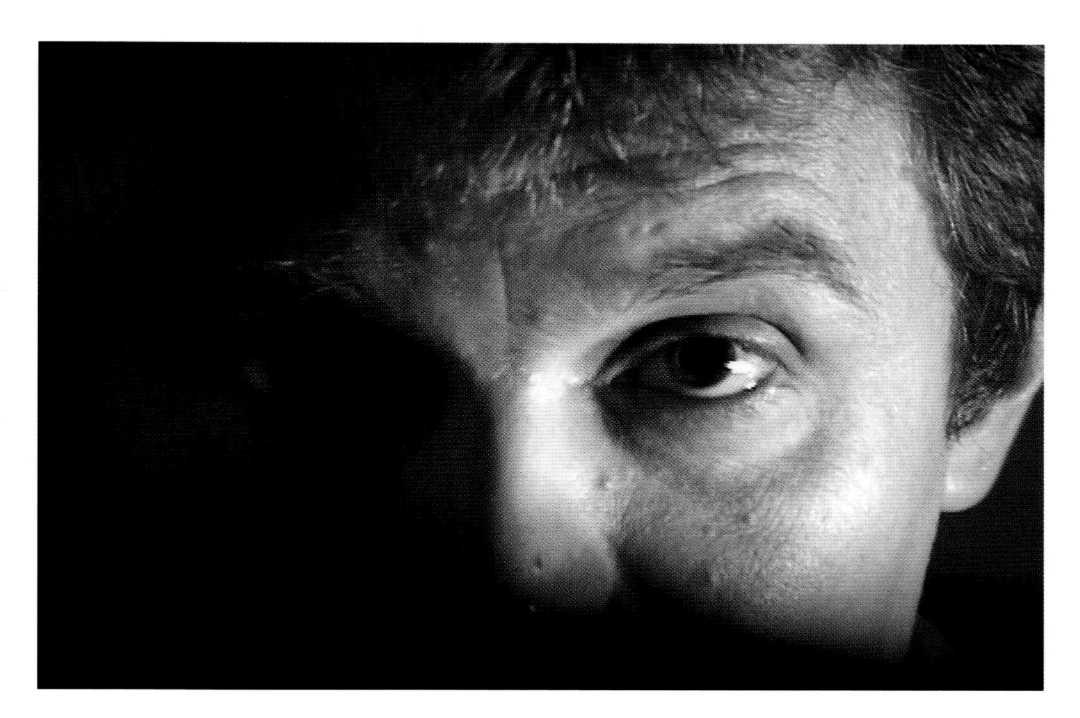

ABOVE Alex Litvinenko was exposed to polonium-210. In three weeks he wasted away with organ failure, and his hair fell out in clumps.

London to take down the "traitor." The particular radioactive signature left behind by the polonium allowed British detectives to trace their route through hotel rooms, restaurants, and boardrooms in London in their hunt for the culprits. The Russians came to London three times in all and possibly made several fumbled attempts on Litvinenko's life. There are even reports that they flew to Hamburg, where they tried to hire an Albanian chef to poison his food.

On November 1, the two Russians and a third, introduced as Vladislav Sokolenko, met Litvinenko at London's Millennium Hotel. A pot of tea was ordered. It came soon after—a white porcelain teapot filled with green tea, with lemon and honey on the side. It is possible that when Litvinenko wasn't watching, a dose of polonium-210 was added to the pot before he had his tea.

Whatever the truth of the matter, later that day he began to feel ill. He firstly had diarrhea and vomiting, and then his hair began to fall out in clumps. His liver and kidneys shut down, and he suffered three massive heart attacks. He died on November 23, 2006, three weeks after the poisoning.

They Had It Coming

Not all assassins do the devil's work. Corrupt, sadistic, or just plain bad individuals sometimes rise to positions of power to spread misery and death throughout their domains. It is hardly surprising that these leaders are assassinated. In a free and fair democratic process, they would soon be voted out of office as their vicious nature repelled the majority of the population. But where democracy does not exist, sometimes the only way to remove these characters is through violent means.

THE MAD MONK'S DEMISE

There are two versions of the death of Grigori Rasputin (1869–1917). One portrays him as a man possessed by the devil who was killed by Russian patriots. The other, revealed by the autopsy, points to a planned, efficient, and brutal political assassination. What is not in question is the fact that the "Mad Monk" Rasputin had brought the Romanov family into disrepute. It could be argued that he was one of the first victims of the media pack.

All who met Rasputin agreed that he had that unique characteristic granted to few people—charisma. He could fix his steely blue eyes on any hapless soul, and they immediately fell under his spell. Proclaiming himself to be a psychic and faith healer, he joined the Khlysty sect. This secret cult had broken away from the Russian Orthodox Church and was rumored to participate in orgies and flagellation.

Rasputin's reputation as a healer preceded him to St. Petersburg and, desperate to save their hemophiliac son, Alexei, the Czar and Czarina invited him into their circle. While not able to heal the boy completely, Rasputin brought some relief to the heir to the Russian throne. This was welcomed in particular by the German-born Czarina, Alexandra, and her approval gave Rasputin an entry into the highest levels of imperial society.

BELOW **Rasputin was often surrounded by females. Rumors of wild orgies abounded. The Tsarina was said to be under his spell.**

ABOVE **Empress Alexandra of Russia. Hemophilia ran in her family, and this was passed to her son Alexei, the heir to the Romanov throne.**

He relished the situation and soon gained a reputation as a ladies' man, marrying several women as he moved around the country. Orgies were reported in salacious detail by the anti-Romanov press. More damaging for the royal family was Rasputin's influence over Alexandra when Nicholas went to the Eastern Front to command the Russian army in 1915. This left Rasputin as a de facto ruler, and ministerial appointments were made at his or the Czarina's whim. This "ministerial hopscotch" created havoc with the war effort, adding to an already chaotic supply situation. Soldiers at the front were forced to fight without the required ammunition or weapons, leading to catastrophic defeats. Rumors of treason abounded. The Czarina was German by birth, and she and her evil advisor were seen as traitors to the Russian cause. Morale was plummeting both on the home front, with the restive urban population, and on the front lines, where Bolshevik agitators campaigned against the Romanov dynasty. While not all the problems were of Rasputin's making, some members of the Russian aristocracy decided to take him out of the equation.

The best-known version of the murder of Rasputin is from Prince Felix Yusupov, who tells a convoluted tale in which the "Mad Monk" is portrayed as an individual of superhuman and devilish powers. Yusupov admitted that his aim was to kill Rasputin, and to that end he lured him to his palace by offering a liaison with his wife, Princess Irina, the beautiful niece of the Czar.

Just before midnight on December 29, 1916, a car with three occupants arrived at the Yusupov palace. Dr. Lazovert was pretending to be Yusupov's chauffeur. The prince was seated in the back of the vehicle with Rasputin, acting as the perfect host. For his special occasion with the lovely Princess Irina, Rasputin had decked himself out in a fine silk blouse embroidered with cornflowers, velvet breeches, and polished boots; he had combed his lank hair, and smelt of soap. He was on his best behavior.

But Rasputin was walking into a trap. Irina was thousands of kilometers away in the Crimea, and in her place were several noble Russians intent on killing Rasputin.

Rather than being an innocent chauffeur, Lazovert was to be the main agent of execution. He had sourced ground cyanide and inserted it into a number of petits four that were arranged to tempt Rasputin. He also dusted the wine glass that was to be used by their victim with the deadly powder.

Yusupov entertained Rasputin in his specially decorated cellar for an hour before Rasputin finally ate several cakes and downed a quantity of wine. The deadly poison, sufficient to kill several men, had no effect beyond causing him to touch his throat as if having difficulty swallowing. This is the first reference to Rasputin's devilish nature. The myth implies that the cunning peasant had been dosing himself with cyanide for many years so as to build up a tolerance in case of an attempted assassination.

Frustrated that Plan A had failed, the desperate assassin went upstairs and borrowed Grand Duke Dmitri Pavlovich's small-caliber Browning pistol. Coming down the stairs, he shot Rasputin twice. The first bullet struck Rasputin in the chest and penetrated the stomach and liver while the second shot hit the fleeing man in the back and penetrated a kidney. Both should have been fatal shots, and Yusupov watched as Rasputin's face twitched in nervous spasms before his body stiffened and became still. Dr. Lazovert declared that death was instantaneous. The conspirators left the room to arrange for the disposal of the corpse but Yusupov stayed behind.

Here, the second proof that Rasputin was the devil's spawn occurred. Yusupov reported:

> *"All of a sudden, I saw the left eye open... A few seconds later his right eyelid began to quiver, then opened. I then saw both eyes—the green eyes of a viper—staring at me with an expression of diabolical hatred."*

Like a rabid dog, Rasputin leapt up, foaming at the mouth and roaring in rage before seizing Yusupov by the throat. The conspirators set upon him but he then stumbled up the stairs and into a courtyard to escape. The other conspirators, hearing the tumult, poured out of the palace. Four more shots, fired into the back of the fleeing monk, were required before he finally fell, lifeless, to the ground.

The assassins then wrapped Rasputin in a rug, bundled him into a car, and threw him off a bridge

BELOW **Felix Yusupov, who was rumored to be homosexual, offered his wife Irina as a lure to attract Rasputin to his doom.**

into the Neva River, presuming that he would sink below the ice and never be seen again. And here emerges the third key element of the Rasputin myth: An alleged autopsy carried out when he was pulled out of the river revealed that there was water in the victim's lungs. This would mean that cyanide, six bullets, and a beating had not been sufficient to kill him off, and he had finally died by drowning—a version of events that perpetuates the image of Rasputin as an evil figure possessed of almost supernatural powers.

The autopsy carried out by Professor Dmitrii Kosorotov when the body was retrieved from the river on January 1, 1917, paints a more disturbing picture. This was not a civilized assassination involving petits four. None were found in his stomach. Nor was any water found in the lungs. He was killed violently and efficiently by a number of enraged men seeking payback for past insults.

It appears that Rasputin was set upon by all of the conspirators as soon as he arrived at the palace. He was given a savage and prolonged beating before being put out of his misery. His neck showed signs of garroting. As he was choked, one of his murderers hacked at his body with a sword, causing a deep wound on the side of his torso. Rasputin's right ear was almost torn from his head and a blow was delivered to the right side of his head with such force that the right eye popped out on to his cheek. It appears that blows from batons or blackjacks rained upon his face and torso as he was subdued. Once pinned to the ground, Rasputin's trousers were torn from him, his legs were forced apart, and his testicles were completely destroyed and flattened by repeated blows from the murderers' batons.

BELOW **This portrait does little to convey Rasputin's piercing blue eyes. He was a charismatic individual who was able to seduce anybody he desired.**

Rasputin must have suffered unimaginable pain before he was put out of his misery. It seems that the initial shots described by Yusupov are the only realistic portion of his story as those two bullets are found in the autopsy. But rather than the six shots fired into the fleeing man's back as he staggered out of the palace, it appears the coup de grâce was delivered by a .455 Webley revolver fired at point-blank range into his temple. This pistol is a heavy-duty piece with tremendous stopping power. Its 11.6mm shell can stop the toughest

ABOVE **A photograph of Grigori Rasputin's body after he was hauled out of the Nevka River. It revealed horrendous injuries inflicted from four hours of beating.**

opponent in his tracks. There is speculation that it was fired by the British secret agent Oswald Rayner. This would indicate that the reason for Rasputin's death was to help keep Russia involved in World War I.

Images of Rasputin's corpse as it was pulled from the river also indicate that his legs and feet were bound. Arriving alive at the palace just before midnight, his corpse was not removed until approximately 4 a.m. It can realistically be presumed that he was bound and beaten for the majority of this time.

The assassins tried to save their empire with this brutal killing, but Rasputin was only a symptom of the rot affecting the Romanov empire, not the cause.

A Jew's Revenge

Herschel Grynszpan was a young Polish–German Jew who decided to pay back the Nazi government for all the suffering it had imposed on his family. The unwitting victim was a minor functionary in the German foreign office, Ernst vom Rath. This killing was the excuse that Hitler was looking for, and the two bullets fired into Rath's abdomen led to an explosion of anti-Semitic violence throughout Germany and Austria.

Grynszpan's life had been all but destroyed by the policies of the Nazi state. His family were originally quite well off, but after years of Nazi discrimination, the young man felt he could take no more and decided on revenge.

Born in March 1921 in Hanover, where his Polish father was a prosperous tailor, Herschel began life in a comfortable environment; but as Nazi anti-Jewish restrictions began to bite after 1933, he became disenchanted with his life in Germany. Barred from many jobs and unable to find work, the sensitive young man sought to migrate to Palestine, but his age and lack of education meant he could not obtain a visa, and he decided to try his luck in France. Herschel's father arranged for him to live with his uncle and aunt, Abraham and Chawa Grynszpan, in Paris. In mid-July 1936, now aged 15, Herschel began his journey there. At the time, he held a valid Polish passport and a German exit visa. Having heard stories that both German and French border officials were denying transit to Jews, he decided to slip into France illegally.

The welcome he expected in France failed to materialize. The turmoil throughout Europe had prompted thousands of refugees to take shelter behind the French border, but the government was tightening its immigration policies and refusing to grant citizenship or visas to the waves of displaced and homeless Jews. Despite the fact that his papers were in order, Grynszpan was ordered to leave France within four days. He could not move back to Germany, as his visa had expired. His Polish passport had also expired, and he was in effect a stateless refugee. Hiding in vacant garrets and avoiding police searches, the young man said of this time:

BELOW **Herschel Feibel Grynszpan, the Polish-Jewish assassin of Ernst vom Rath. His action was just the excuse the Nazis wanted to turn on the Jews.**

"Being a Jew is not a crime. I am not a dog. I have a right to live and the Jewish people have a right to exist on this earth. Wherever I have been I have been chased like an animal."

It is possible that Herschel took up sex work during this time, and he was known to frequent homosexual clubs.

Herschel had had enough. When he heard that all Polish Jews had been deported back to Poland, he decided to act. Poland at the time was almost as anti-Semitic as the Nazis, and the Polish decree in October 1938 threatened to strip all Polish Jews living in Germany of their citizenship. The Germans, fearing they would have 17,000 stateless Hebrews forced upon them, loaded them all on trains and transported them to the Polish border under the tender care of the Gestapo. Polish border guards were taken by surprise and refused to admit the poor refugees. Thousands of

once-prosperous families were stranded in no man's land between the two countries, living outdoors in the chilly autumn weather or sheltering in abandoned buildings.

Herschel's worst fears were realized when he received a tearful letter from his sister explaining that his family was in a desperate plight, stuck on the border and asking for money. Three days after receiving this letter, on November 7, Herschel Grynszpan wrote a farewell letter to his parents, bought a revolver and ammunition, and made his way to the German Embassy in Paris. He asked, as a German citizen, to see an Embassy official. Ernst vom Rath was free and politely approached the young man, whereupon Grynszpan whipped out his revolver and drilled two bullets into Vom Rath's guts.

ABOVE **The funeral of Ernst vom Rath. This minor diplomatic functionary was turned into a Nazi martyr, and his death was used to incite Kristallnacht.**

The injured official was immediately evacuated to Germany where the best medical care could not save him. He was given a state funeral in Düsseldorf, attended by Adolf Hitler and foreign minister Joachim von Ribbentrop.

From November 1938 to June 1940, Herschel was imprisoned by the French in Fresnes Prison near Paris, before being moved to the prison in Toulouse. On July 18,

Night of the Broken Glass

In response to this assassination, in the late evening of November 9, 1938, the Nazis began a systematic attack on Jews in Germany. The event was named *Kristallnacht* ("night of crystal") in reference to all the broken glass that littered the German streets after thousands of shops and houses belonging to Jews had their windows broken. SA and SS troops in plain clothes, and with the approval of the Nazi leadership, embarked on an orgy of destruction and looting. Jewish property was systematically smashed and burned. Over 90 people were killed, 1,000 Jewish shops and businesses were looted, and 191 synagogues were burned down. During the next week, over 20,000 Jewish men and boys were rounded up and placed in concentration camps. Organized warfare against the Jewish population had begun.

Foreign observers were shocked by the naked hatred displayed by many Germans. Michael Bruce, an Englishman, provided this eyewitness account:

"By now the streets were a chaos of screaming bloodthirsty people lusting for Jewish bodies. I saw Harrison of The News Chronicle, *trying to protect an aged Jewess who had been dragged from her home by a gang. I pushed my way through to help him and, between us, we managed to heave her through the crowd to a side street and safety."*

BELOW **One of the 191 burned during Kristallnacht, Ohel Yaaqov Synagogue remained derelict as a symbol of Nazi vengeance.**

a month after the German occupation, he was flown to Berlin and locked up in the Gestapo headquarters at Prinz-Albrecht-Strasse. He was held in German custody in a number of Gestapo institutions, including Moabit Prison in Berlin, and Flossenburg and Sachsenhausen concentration camps.

Goebbels' propaganda ministry initially planned a show trial to condemn the young man and no doubt sentence him to death. These plans were quietly shelved when it was learned that Vom Rath frequented homosexual haunts, and Grynszpan's lawyer was set to argue that the shots had been fired as the result of a lover's tiff.

Grynszpan's fate is unknown but it is likely he was beaten to death by the Gestapo or SS. He was declared legally dead by German authorities in the 1960s.

Death of a Killer

Himmler's deputy, Reinhard Heydrich, was a pathological killer who struck terror into many who found themselves fixed in his lizard-like gaze. He became one of the main architects of the police state throughout the occupied territories as well as one of the key architects of the "Final Solution," Hitler's plan to annihilate all Jews in Europe.

Obergruppenführer Heydrich always drove to his Prague headquarters in an open-topped Mercedes, without armed outriders, and usually with the hood retracted. This was to demonstrate the power he had over his subjects, and he continued this practice against advice from his colleagues. On May 27, 1942, as the vehicle turned a bend, it came under attack from British-trained Czech and Slovak patriots. Wounded by bullets and shrapnel, he died eight days later. Upholstery from the car's seats and fragments of his uniform were lodged in his guts, where they turned septic and led to blood poisoning.

ABOVE Reinhard Heydrich just before his assassination. Leather upholstery lodged in his guts turned septic and led to his death.

The decision to assassinate Heydrich was taken by the British espionage agency in October 1941, and the operation was code-named "Anthropoid." The definition of an anthropoid is a creature that mimics humans or is a lower form of hominid, such as an ape—perhaps a statement on Heydrich's chillingly cold demeanor.

The operation was planned by the British Special Operations Executive (SOE), which was formed by Churchill to destabilize the Nazi regime through subversion and sabotage that would "set Europe ablaze." Several Czech operatives went through intensive training in bomb making, parachute insertions, hand-to-hand combat, sabotage, and camouflage. Their training placed special emphasis on how to use sensitive timers and fuses, and it was this aspect that allowed them to take down Heydrich. Josef Gabčík and Jan Kubiš were chosen to carry out the assassination after several mishaps involving other trainees.

The two men signed their last will and testament and were flown to the continent, with a support team of wireless operators, in a Halifax bomber. The heavily laden assassins parachuted out and landed near a small village called Lidice, east of Prague, just before the New Year. This later led to tragic consequences for the rural hamlet.

The two men and their support team had enough in their arsenal to take out the entire Nazi hierarchy. They had two pistols, a .38 Colt (with four full spare magazines and 100 bullets), six armor-piercing bombs filled with plastic explosives, two magazines of fuses, two model Mills grenades, one Tree Spigot bomb launcher with one bomb, four electric fuses, one Sten Mk.II machine gun with 100 bullets, 32 pounds (14.5 kilograms) of plastic explosives, two yards of fuse rope, four smoke bombs, a reel of steel string, and three timing pencils.

Going underground, the two men made contact with a few select resistance groups and began to plan the time and place of the operation. For six months they lay low, looking for the perfect opportunity to carry out their strike. During this time, some Czech agencies were in touch with the government in exile, trying to get the operation cancelled. The people of Prague

BELOW **German soldiers standing by corpses after the mass execution of all the men in Lidice, Czechoslovakia, June 1942. They died as revenge for Heydrich.**

ABOVE **Operation Reinhard was named in Heydrich's honor. It saw millions of people killed in four extermination camps.**

knew how ruthless the Germans could be, and they feared the consequences of a successful attempt on Heydrich's life. They were correct, and almost 5,000 innocent victims died as a result of Gestapo payback.

Several attempts were planned to carry out the operation but each time they came unstuck. However, the agents did note two things that gave cause for optimism. The first was Heydrich's preference to drive without an escort with his Mercedes' hood down, a demonstration that he was in total control of his Czech fiefdom. The second chink in the armor was that Heydrich's route into the capital from his country estate took him through a hairpin bend and forced his chauffeur to slow to a crawl, creating an excellent target of opportunity. Adjacent to this bend was a tram stop. The assassins could stand out in the open as if they were waiting for a tram, rather than waiting to kill.

Then came bad news. Whispers came down to the team that all their hard work building up an idea of Heydrich's movements might be wasted. Their target was returning to Germany and possibly reassigned to another office. However, the conspirators had a piece of luck and found out exactly where he would be on May 27, 1942. Marie Rasnerova, an operative in the resistance, worked as a cleaner in Heydrich's headquarters. She pulled a copy of his itinerary out of the wastepaper basket and passed the valuable document to Kubiš and Gabčík. They now knew in detail which routes Heydrich would take. He would be going through the hairpin bend on the way to Hradcany Castle.

Early in the morning of the 27th, Kubiš was in position with his bombs while Gabčík waited with his locked and loaded Sten submachine gun. The plan was that Gabčík's girlfriend, who owned a car, would drive in front of Heydrich's car, and if he was unescorted she would wear a hat to indicate that he was a live target. Another operative was positioned so that he could peer around the corner and indicate with a signaling mirror when Heydrich's Mercedes was actually approaching. As Heydrich entered the bend and slowed, Gabčík's role was to open up with his machine gun and kill him and his driver, while Kubiš snatched Heydrich's briefcase.

At first it seemed something had gone awry. The assassins waited at the tram stop right through the morning peak period, and as the crowds dispersed they began to worry that they would appear too obvious, standing in the same position hour after hour. But at 10:31 a.m. sharp, Gabčík's girl drove round the bend. She was wearing a hat. Seconds later, the mirror's signal came. With a pounding heart, Gabčík stepped forward into the middle of the road, waiting for his prey. Heydrich's Mercedes came into view and Gabčík pulled the trigger, but some grass had got into the gun's sensitive breech and it failed to fire.

Bullies are usually cowards but Heydrich proved the exception to the rule. Seeing the impudent Czech standing in the middle of the road aiming a submachine gun at him, he ordered his chauffeur to stop, pulled his pistol, and shot back at his attacker. Kubiš, seeing his comrade in danger, drew his sensitive impact fused bomb and lobbed it at the car. The custom-built fuse detonated the bomb near the car, shattering Heydrich's rear door. As shrapnel and upholstery ripped through his body, Heydrich remained standing and even climbed out of the vehicle to pursue his fleeing attackers. Kubiš was hit in the face and eyes by shrapnel splinters but managed to get on his cycle and ride off, pursued by Klein, the SS driver. They thought the attempt was a failure, unaware of the severity of Heydrich's wounds.

Heydrich staggered a few paces from the car as he tried to apprehend the attackers, but then collapsed. He was taken to a hospital, and there, at first, it was thought his

LEFT Jan Kubiš and Jozef Gabčík were tasked with killing Heydrich. The two men signed their last wills and testaments before being parachuted into occupied Europe.

wounds were not serious; an X-ray revealed a broken rib and some fragments of cloth and metal in his stomach. These fragments would prove to be his undoing, as they turned his wounds septic. In addition, pieces of burned leather upholstery and uniform cloth were buried near the spleen, and other small fragments embedded in the pleura.

Heydrich was taken to Bulovka Hospital, near the site of the attack. There he was operated on by Professor Hollbaum, a Silesian German who was Chairman of Surgery at Charles University in Prague, assisted by Doctor Dick, the Sudeten German Chief of Surgery at the hospital. The surgeons reinflated the collapsed left lung, removed the tip of the fractured eleventh rib, sutured the torn diaphragm, inserted several catheters, and removed the spleen, which contained a grenade fragment and upholstery material. The best medical care was employed, as other specialists were flown in from Germany, and it seemed the terror supremo might pull through.

But on June 4, Heydrich died—not directly of his wounds, but of gangrene and septicemia. There were rumors that he had been showing signs of recovery, but some rivals within the Gestapo were quite pleased with the assassins' work and might have added poison to his medication, or perhaps he was just smothered with a pillow.

LEFT **This statue to commemorate Operation Anthropod honors the Czech resistance as well as the British involvement.**

ABOVE **The state funeral of Reinhard Heydrich, June 9, 1942. Rumors persist that enemies in the Nazi party "facilitated" his death.**

Heydrich's corpse was dressed in his black SS uniform, which had struck terror into thousands of people. He was placed in a coffin of gunmetal and silver before being taken in a special train for his funeral in Berlin.

Straight after the attack, the Gestapo started hunting the assassins. Their first tip-off came when a traitor provided an extensive list of those who had helped the SOE-trained operatives. The very next morning, the Gestapo began extended raids on the apartments of the people who had assisted the paratroopers. The first in line was the Moravec family in Biskupcova Street in Prague. The family was made to stand in the corridor while the Gestapo searched their apartment. Mrs. Moravec was allowed to go to the bathroom, and killed herself with a cyanide capsule. Mr. Moravec and his son, Ata, were taken into custody and tortured. Mr Moravec could not give any information, as he was not involved in the plot. Ata held out until he was forced to drink copious amounts of brandy before being shown his mother's decapitated head in a fish tank. He spilled the beans.

That night, June 18, several SS battalions surrounded the Church of St. Cyril and Methodius. Kubiš and Gabčík were hiding there with other paratroopers, waiting for the heat to die down. The Nazis launched an attack but were held off for 14 hours by the desperate defenders, who were eventually forced into the crypt of the church. The only access to the crypt from the street was via a small ventilation opening in the western part of the church. The Germans seized this opportunity and ordered in the Prague fire department to begin flooding the crypt with water and tear gas.

Near the altar, under a carpet, the Germans found another entrance to the crypt, covered with a stone slab. After destroying it with explosives, they discovered steep stairs leading into the crypt. The Czech assassins were now fighting from all sides.

The remaining defenders, exhausted and their ammunition just about gone, chose suicide over capture. Josef Gabčík ended his own life with a pistol shot. The dead paratroopers were carried out in front of the church and identified by the traitor, Karel Čurda.

The Nazi reckoning was savage. More than 1,000 individuals who had even the loosest association with the assassins were murdered in Gestapo cells. Thousands of Jews were rounded up and sent to the Theresienstadt camp-ghetto. In other camps and prisons in the Reich, innocents were killed in bloody, senseless retributions. Even worse, several villages in the Czech protectorate, including Lidice, were levelled while the men were killed and the rest of the population shipped to extermination camps. Hitler's final revenge was to name the Final Solution "Operation Rheinhard" after his ruthless subordinate. Millions died in the extermination camps of Sobibor, Balzec, and Treblinka.

Apartheid Architect

Few individuals have caused so much suffering as Hendrik Verwoerd (1901–1966). Born in the Netherlands, he began life as a son of religious shopkeepers. The family moved to South Africa and the young Hendrik soon proved to be an able scholar, gaining a doctorate at the University of Stellenbosch. However, during this time, he also developed a fierce hatred for the British due to their actions in the Boer War. He turned down a position at Oxford and instead went to Germany to complete his studies.

While there, he picked up on the racially charged atmosphere of 1920s' Germany; and he was studying under the anthropologist Dr. Eugen Fischer, who advocated anti-Semitism, racial segregation, and genocide.

In 1927, Verwoerd returned to South Africa, bringing with him all the hatred and prejudices he had picked up in Germany. He found the perfect vehicle to disseminate his radical agenda when, as editor of the newspaper *Die Transvaler*, he wrote articles that were anti-Semitic and criticized mixed marriages while advocating the adoption of race laws such as those passed by the German Nazis.

During the 1950s, as a minister and, by 1958, the prime minister of the newly established Republic of South Africa, Verwoerd and his right-wing National Party put

ABOVE South African Prime Minister Hendrik Verwoerd, 1961. He spent time studying in Nazi Germany, and this influenced his policy of apartheid.

his crackpot theories into practice. Thousands of blacks were forced into black homelands (Bantustans) and black-only townships such as Soweto. Poor sanitation and overcrowding were characteristic of these squalid settlements. Stripped of the right of universal education, the original African inhabitants were only allowed basic educations, to suit their future as underpaid menials. Blacks were not allowed to vote, were subject to police brutality and arbitrary arrest, and had at all times to carry pass books—known as dompas, the "dumb pass"—restricting their free movement around the country. Mixed-race sexual relations were deemed a criminal act, citizenship was revoked from many black communities, and of course only whites were able to compete in national sporting teams.

As the creator of such a monstrous system, it might be thought that Verwoerd would have been the target of an assassin with political motives, but this was not the case. On September 6, 1966, the prime minister entered the House of Assembly. He was approached by a parliamentary messenger who pulled a sheath knife on Verwoerd, raised his arm, and stabbed him four times in the chest. Many parliamentarians had a medical background, and they came from all directions to save the stricken politician, but all to no avail. Upon arrival at Groote Schuur Hospital, Verwoerd was declared DOA (dead on arrival). The knife had done its work and punctured the lungs and the heart.

The assassin was 48-year-old Dimitri Tsafendas who, although he was categorized "white" under the classification system, was in fact dark-skinned. This meant that he was taunted by white colleagues but could not live with his black girlfriend. The situation tipped the already unstable man into madness, and he was convinced there was a giant tapeworm in his body that talked to him and told him to kill Verwoerd. He was confined in a psychiatric hospital until his death in 1999.

THE FIRST "SELFIE" KILLING

Just as Archduke Franz Ferdinand's assassination was the first multimedia execution, Muammar Gaddafi's gruesome death was the first "selfie" killing, with many participants recording the events on their mobile phones. After he received a bullet in the head, hundreds of freedom fighters posed for "selfies" with the dead dictator.

Muammar Gaddafi was born to a Bedouin family in Sirte, Libya, on June 7, 1942. In 1963, he joined King Idris' military academy and began a steady rise through the ranks. His promotion schedule sped up when, during September 1969, he led a movement to overthrow the king and at 27 years of age became the Commander in Chief of the Libyan Army as a newly promoted colonel, as well as Chairman of Libya's new governing body, the Revolutionary Command Council. In these roles, he served as dictator of Libya for more than 40 years. One of his key actions was to make political dissent a capital crime in 1969.

His revolution began in a promising manner with the oil-rich nation regaining control of its vast petroleum fields and Gaddafi redirecting much of the wealth to Libya's citizens. But as the years went by, he became increasingly unstable, and by promoting his unique philosophy through his "Green Book" he ruled his country with increasingly violent methods.

He became a sexual predator and would visit schools and select teenage girls and boys by patting them on the head. They would then be hauled off and trained to become his sexual playthings. Many of the women were initiated into his crack "women's brigade" where they were asked to perform or witness executions. Opponents were assassinated by one of several teams he employed to enforce his will, and many of his victims were brought to one of Gaddafi's palaces, where their bodies were literally stored on ice so he could come and gloat over their frozen corpses whenever the fancy took him.

RIGHT **Muammar Gaddafi began his murderous career at the age of 27 when he led an armed coup that threw out the Libyan king in 1969.**

ABOVE **President of Libya, Muammar Gaddafi, 2008. He is surrounded by his crack Women's Brigade that provided sex and security to the dictator.**

Gaddafi declared himself to be King of Africa and sought to promote himself on the world stage. He became involved in conflicts in Chad, Northern Ireland, and the Sudan, contributing to at least a million deaths. He alienated many in the West when his agents allegedly brought down a jumbo jet over Lockerbie, Scotland, in 1988. A total of 259 people died in the plane, and 11 civilians were killed by falling debris. (After this terrorist attack, new security measures were brought in to international flights. It is no longer possible to check in luggage and then not get on the flight. Anyone who is a no-show has their luggage removed.)

Despite his posturing on the world stage, Libyans became increasingly disenchanted with Gaddafi's ruthless plundering of his country's assets, and when the "Arab Spring" of 2011 forced out Tunisia's and Egypt's dictators, demonstrations broke out throughout Libya. After six months' fighting, and with NATO air support, the rebels had seized most of Libya and proclaimed themselves to be the National Transitional Council (NTC).

However, Gaddafi and his last loyalist supporters still held out in his hometown of Sirte, which he renamed the capital of Libya. But not for long. By October, rebels were closing in on the stronghold and Gaddafi sought to flee to a neighboring country in a convoy of up to 70 vehicles.

The armed convoy was packed with the last of the dictator's loyal supporters. NATO drones soon fixed its location and fighter bombers strafed the convoy while rebel forces closed in. At least 20 vehicles were destroyed and 55 men died in the initial strike. The remaining vehicles scattered in an attempt to evade the encircling rebels. It was not to be and many of Gaddafi's diehard supporters were captured and killed out of hand while trying to break through the rebel cordon.

Gaddafi and his immediate bodyguard took refuge on a building site, and while his henchmen sought to keep off the rebels, the dictator hid in a drainage pipe. It is likely that during this time he was wounded in the thigh with shrapnel, while his left ear or scalp also suffered a wound, causing blood to pour all over his head and chest.

Finally, his last bodyguards were eliminated, and Gaddafi was hauled out of his temporary shelter. Dragged on to the bonnet of a rebel "technical" (a pickup truck adapted for military use), the "King of Africa" begged for mercy with the words "What did I do to you?" In a moment captured on camera, some rebels climbed on to the hood and kicked him, while others beat him and tried to strip his clothing. All around the stricken man, rebels fired off Kalashnikovs into the air while he begged and cried for his life. In one film, a young man leapt on to the vehicle and addressed the guards: "Gaddafi must be kept alive for trial," he argued.

Once again, just as the fatal shots fired by Gavrilo Princip at the Archduke Franz Ferdinand were not photographed, the few seconds when Gaddafi was executed by a pistol bullet in the head and one in the stomach are not recorded. He is next shown as a lifeless corpse being dragged into an ambulance. There's no dignity in death, and he is shown as an old potbellied man with his pants falling below his waist. Fighters lift his head and drop it, showing that despite his half-open eyes, Muammar Gaddafi is truly dead.

Muslim law decrees that the deceased must be buried within 24 hours. Instead, the tyrant was displayed in a local businessman's freezer, along with the corpse of his son and heir, Mutassim. He too had been assassinated soon after capture. Over the next week, thousands of Libyans traveled from all over the country to view their chilled corpses.

Gaddafi's Golden Pistol

Gaddafi and his family were known for their collections of personal weapons. The best known were their gold-plated Kalashnikovs, similar to the ones owned by fellow dictator Saddam Hussein. Gaddafi also possessed a golden 9mm Browning automatic. It was initially reported that this was the weapon used to shoot the dictator, but this soon proved to be inaccurate. The young rebel who found it later reported that he had gone to inspect the shot-up convoy and found it lying in the sand. It turned into something of a mixed blessing. He was offered $385,000 for the souvenir but also received numerous death threats from surviving regime loyalists.

CHAPTER 5 THE PRICE OF FAME

SOME OF THE MORE FORTUNATE AMONG US are able to rise to the pinnacle of fame through a combination of talent, connections, and good luck. These lucky few can be worldwide iconic figures or famous within their country. With fame comes great fortune and adulation from devoted fans. But not all gifts of fame are positive. An intrusive media makes life unbearable for some, while obsessed fans cross the line from admirers to stalkers. In some instances, unbalanced fans fixate on their idols and become ruthless murderers.

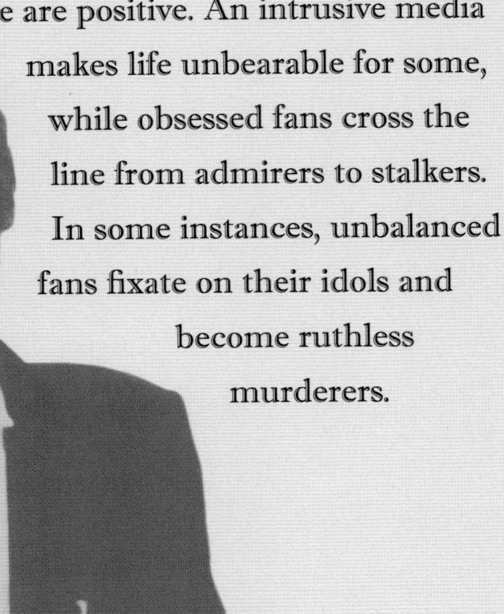

Back From the Dead

Andy Warhol had two shots fired into his lungs by the radical feminist and ex-prostitute Valerie Solanas. After Warhol had refused to produce one of her diatribes against males, she vowed payback. On June 3, 1968, she walked into Warhol's New York studio, "The Factory," armed with a .32 caliber pistol. Almost twenty years later, Warhol died as a result of the wounds she inflicted.

The artistic "enfant terrible" was born into a nondescript household of Slovakian working-class migrants. He had both Jewish and Catholic ancestors. From an early age, he displayed a precocious artistic talent and a rebellious streak. He studied commercial art and in 1949 moved to New York to begin a career as a magazine illustrator, specializing in producing advertising copy.

In the 1960s Warhol began his campaigns of attacking the art establishment and promoting his own personality cult. He began to attack the concept that fine art represented values and understandings only available to the elite within society, and that each piece of fine art has to be unique and valuable. He sought to prove that art could be mass-produced and made in factory-like conditions. His pictures of soup cans and colorized portraits of Marilyn Monroe may be seen as icons of 20th-century art, but it is doubtful they would be held in such regard were it not for the celebrity status of their producer.

It was fortunate for Warhol that he began his activities in the 1960s when American society was being challenged by a younger

BELOW Andy Warhol's *Campbell's Soup Cans*. He produced his best work in his studio, "The Factory."

generation eager to embrace new ideas. Warhol's studio on Union Square, nicknamed "The Factory," attracted hundreds of celebrities as well as artistic wannabes. It was just his bad luck that it attracted one deranged feminist, determined to get a bit of payback against the patriarchy.

Valerie Solanas was born in April 1936 and was abused by her father until she became homeless at the age of 15. Nevertheless, she managed to put herself through Maryland University, earning a degree in psychology. During the late 1950s and early 60s, she led a shiftless, rootless existence, living on the fringes of society and earning income as a part-time prostitute.

BELOW **Portrait of Andy Warhol, who was attacked in 1968 by radical feminist Valerie Solanas.**

As her mental health deteriorated during these years, so her hatred of men intensified. Solanas founded, and was the sole member of, a radical feminist sect called SCUM (Society for Cutting Up Men). The organization's constitution avowed that its aim was to eliminate all men from the surface of the earth and replace them with machines that would fulfill all of their functions, including reproductive acts. The troubled woman declared herself a playwright and offered a script to Warhol, with whom she had formed a loose association, hoping that he would produce it. Warhol's activities were already being monitored by some government agencies, and he thought that the play "Up Your Ass" was too over the top.

Solanas was not one to take no for an answer, and after purchasing a cheap pistol, she marched into Warhol's studio with murder in her heart. Warhol was on the phone, and she fired three rounds at the unsuspecting artist. Two missed, but one bullet was almost mortal. It tore through both lungs and his spleen, stomach, and liver before bursting out adjacent to his esophagus. The assassin then turned the pistol on the art critic Mario Amaya, wounding him in the thigh. She had plenty of anger left over and turned to Warhol's manager, Fred Hughes, aimed at his head, and pulled the trigger. Fortunately for Hughes, the pistol jammed and Solanas fled the studio.

Warhol was taken to hospital and declared DOA (dead on arrival). However, in a last desperate attempt to save the famous artist, his chest was cut open, and open heart massage was administered. After several minutes, some vital signs returned, and surgeons embarked on a marathon five-and-a-half-hour operation. During this time, Warhol's spleen was removed, and the gaping wound in his throat where the bullet had exited was stitched. Nevertheless, he was still in a critical condition, and he spent more than two months in intensive care, quietly mending. For the rest of his life, Warhol was plagued by long-term damage inflicted by that one bullet. A corset was required to hold his guts in place, and the wounds often reopened and bled if he over-exerted himself.

The most significant effect on the "genius" was to instill a lifelong fear of hospitals in his psyche. He had recurring gallbladder problems but put off going to hospital. Warhol was convinced that if he ever entered hospital again he would die. He was right. In February 1987, he turned up for surgery at New York Hospital, but on the 22nd he died in his sleep from complications. He was 58 when he died but would probably have lived longer if it were not for the attack.

Solanas surrendered soon after the shooting but spent only three years in jail after pleading guilty to first-degree assault. Her victims refused to give evidence against her. When released, she reverted to her life of part-time prostitution combined with panhandling (begging) before dying of pneumonia one year after Warhol.

A Star Falls

At 10:50 p.m. on December 8, 1980, John Lennon and his wife, Yoko Ono, got out of a limousine in front of their apartment building in New York after returning from a recording session. Lennon locked eyes with a young fan who hours earlier had requested the ex-Beatle to sign an album. As the pair turned away and walked into the foyer of their building, The Dakota, located on the corner of 72nd and Central Park West, the young man, now known as Mark Chapman, pulled out a .38 caliber handgun from his pocket and shot at Lennon five times.

Mark David Chapman was born in May 1955 in Fort Worth, Texas. His father was in the air force, and the family moved to Atlanta, Georgia. Chapman was not popular at school and was frequently bullied. To cope with rejections from his peers, the young man developed a rich fantasy life that caused obsessional interests in different topics. An overuse of drugs in his early teens was followed by a period as an evangelical Christian. One of his dominant interests throughout this whole period was an unhealthy fascination with John Lennon.

BELOW **Yoko Ono and John Lennon. The two were devoted to each other, and Yoko Ono was there in Lennon's last moments.**

CHAPMAN THRUST THE ALBUM FORWARD AND LENNON, IN GOOD SPIRITS, SIGNED IT AND ASKED IF CHAPMAN WANTED ANYTHING ELSE. CHAPMAN WAS ENTRANCED AND HE ALMOST DECIDED TO RETURN HOME WITH HIS PRECIOUS PRIZE.

During the 1970s and 80s, Chapman became mentally disturbed, paranoid, and depressed. He considered suicide and made several failed attempts. One of these involved trying to gas himself in his car, but the plastic pipe attached to the exhaust melted before he became unconscious.

As Chapman spiraled into madness, he became influenced by two books: *The Catcher in the Rye* and *John Lennon: One Day at a Time*. The first glorified the mentally unstable Holden Caulfield, while the second preached Lennon's rather hypocritical take on the virtues of a simple life uncluttered by wealth and material goods. Crucially, the latter title informed Chapman that Lennon was currently living in New York, and once he had this information the young obsessive fan formed a plan to kill his idol.

Mark Chapman was something of a rarity in that he was fully aware of the mental issues he suffered. With schizophrenic and bipolar tendencies, he knew that much of his thinking was delusional and was constantly embroiled in internal conflicts as he tried to hang on to his sanity. The day that Chapman killed Lennon, December 8, 1980, was no different. The killer oscillated between hero worship of the musician and a desire to kill him.

Using money borrowed from a relative, Chapman arrived in New York on Saturday, December 6, determined to meet his idol. He bought a copy of Lennon's latest release, "Double Fantasy," and hung around the entrance of the Dakota building waiting to see the musician. He was unsuccessful but returned the next day. Once again, he failed to meet Lennon. Chapman had some of his borrowed money left and booked into the posh Sheraton Hotel. As if somehow aware that it would be his last night of freedom, the disturbed young man splashed out on some luxuries. This included a booking with a high-end call girl. Like his hero, Holden Caulfield, he just wanted her for conversation and after chewing her ear for several hours he allowed her to leave at 3 a.m. with $190 in her pocket.

The next morning, Chapman grabbed his newly acquired album and his gun and headed back to the Dakota building. This day was more fruitful. He met Lennon's son, the five-year-old Sean, and shook the boy's hand. Several hours later, John and Yoko exited the building. Chapman thrust the album forward and Lennon, in good spirits, signed it and asked if Chapman wanted anything else. Chapman was entranced and he almost decided to return home with his precious prize.

He wrangled with himself, but his evil destructive demons took over. Chapman determined to go through with his plan to assassinate Lennon and decided to stay at the apartment's foyer, lurking outside, reading a recently purchased copy of Salinger's classic novel and waiting for his target. At 10:50 p.m. John and Yoko returned in their white limousine. John stepped out and looked at the young man, seeming to recognize him from their earlier encounter. He walked on with Yoko. Chapman made up his mind, a sinister voice in his head repeating over and over again, "Do it, do it, do it." He pulled the gun out of his pocket and carried out his dark desires.

Armed with the Charter Arms .38 special, he crouched down into a combat stance, yelled "Mr. Lennon," and fired off five lethal hollow-point bullets. One shot missed, passing over his target's head, but the other four shots, fired at point-blank range, smashed into Lennon's back where they partially disintegrated, shredding Lennon's internal organs. All were to the left of his spine; two went into his shoulder and two into his back. Any of them could have been mortal but all four combined meant there was no hope for the musician. Chapman's victim tried to flee from the gun and managed to run forward six paces. Then he fell forward, uttering the words "I'm shot." The last words he would ever utter.

Chapman's shooting had been spectacularly successful. The bullets had hit in a lethal cluster around Lennon's heart, cutting his arteries and shredding his aorta. One lodged next to his heart, and one was embedded in his shoulder, while the other two virtually vaporized his lungs as they burst through his chest wall. An on-the-spot EU (Emergency Unit) could not have saved him.

The building's concierge, Jay Hastings, had noticed Chapman lurking in the shadows of the building's grand entrance moments before the attack. He ran to Lennon's assistance and turned him over amid the scattered cassettes dropped by the musician as he fell. Hastings sought to make a tourniquet, but seeing the seriousness of the wounds, he then tried to staunch the blood by taking off his jacket and pressing it over the wounds.

Two police officers arrived and, seeing the seriousness of the situation, decided not to call an ambulance but picked up the stricken man and placed him in their squad car before turning on their sirens and lights and racing to nearby St Luke's Hospital Centre. One of the officers asked "Are you John Lennon?" but all he got was a gurgle and a wheeze in reply as blood continued to pour from the multiple gunshot wounds.

Dr. Stephan Lynn had just got off a 13-hour shift as head of emergency when, a minute or two before 11 p.m., he heard a commotion in the corridor. Seconds later two police officers, one with a bloody Lennon over his shoulder, rounded a corner yelling that they had John Lennon who had multiple gunshot wounds and no vital signs.

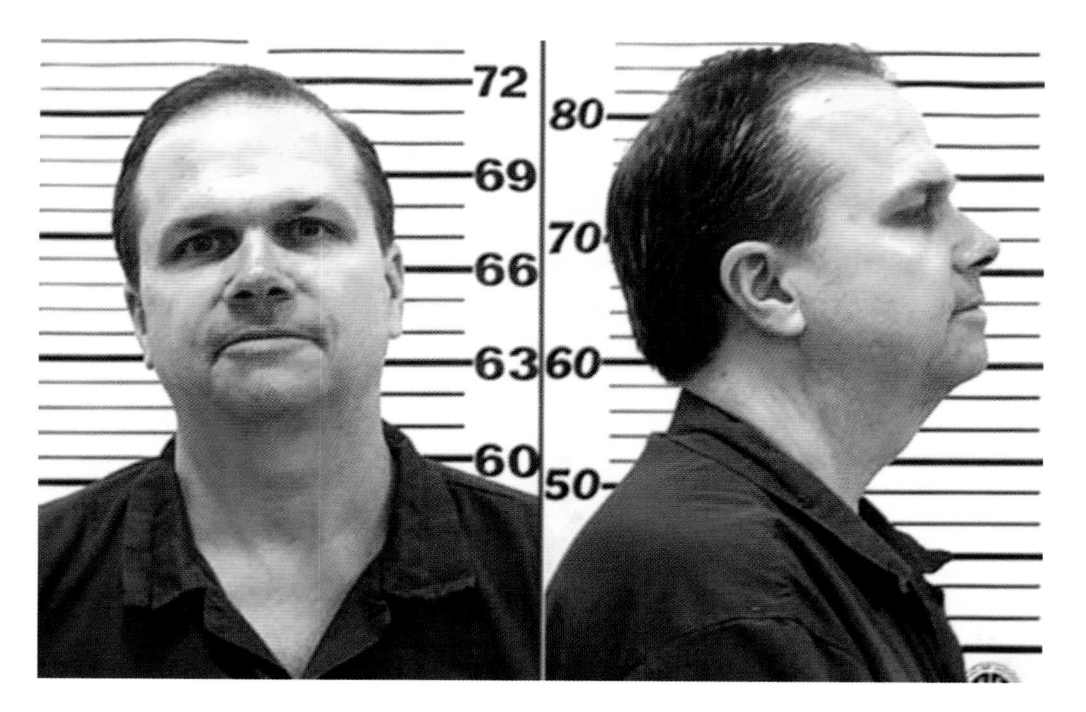

ABOVE **Mugshot of Mark Chapman. The killer sat calmly reading a book after firing fatal shots at John Lennon.**

A mere 30 seconds later the unresponsive Lennon, who had no pulse or blood pressure, was having his chest cut open as Lynn placed his hand around his heart and tried to massage the organ back to life. Blood was administered, but it poured out as soon as it was pumped in. Most of the wounds were around the arteries and heart. After 20 minutes of frantic lifesaving efforts, John Lennon was pronounced dead at 11:15 p.m. The cause of death was officially reported as "hypovolemic shock" caused by more than 80 percent blood loss.

Straight after the shooting, Mark Chapman had the gun wrestled out of his hands by the Dakota's doorman, who then went to help the stricken Lennon. Two minutes later, police arrived and found Chapman sitting very calmly, his coat over his knees, reading his copy of J.D. Salinger's *The Catcher in the Rye*. Chapman was cuffed before being bundled into the back of a patrol car.

Chapman has given many reasons for deciding to kill the superstar. Many are ridiculous. Perhaps he was closest to the truth when he apologized for the action in a parole hearing 20 years after the crime, saying "I did it for the attention." He is still in prison, despite repeated parole hearings.

Wrapped-Up Rappers

The Notorious B.I.G. was hit by four bullets at 12:45 on the morning of March 9, 1997. He was sitting in the passenger seat of a black SUV halted at an intersection in downtown L.A. Behind him was another vehicle packed with Bloods bodyguards.

Another vehicle drove up and took station next to the rapper's car. The window slid down, and in what seemed to be a split second, six rounds were discharged at the rapper's large frame. One lodged in the door, one went through the vehicle to exit on the other side. The other four slammed into their target. Three were flesh wounds. One was lethal.

If Notorious B.I.G. hadn't ducked for cover, he'd still be alive. The first bullet hit the rapper's right elbow and traveled down to his wrist—a flesh wound. One went through his right thigh, missing any arterial veins—a flesh wound. Next, he was hit in the back. The bullet went under the skin, exiting out of the left shoulder—a flesh wound.

B.I.G. was probably upright when these bullets hit—but he was lying over his driver's lap, trying to dodge down, when the fourth and final bullet hit. That instinctive reaction killed him. The fatal bullet entered just above the right hip and ripped straight through the middle of his prone body. It

BELOW **A mural of the Notorious B.I.G. in New York. He was affiliated with several New York gangs, and this led to his assassination.**

pulverized his colon and smashed into his liver before punching through the right atrium of his heart, then the left ventricle, and finally exiting out of his left shoulder.

The shooter's car took off. B.I.G. was rushed to nearby Cedar Sinai Medical Center. To all appearances, it seemed he would survive, as there was apparently little blood loss. In fact, B.I.G.'s bulk had occluded the bullet holes, preventing external bleeding. Inside was a different matter. Blood poured from his shattered heart, filling up his internal cavities. Had the bullet gone 2 centimeters (1 inch) to the left or right, he would have lived.

Death was declared at 1:15 a.m., 20 minutes after he arrived at Sinai. His assassination mirrored almost exactly the attack on his biggest rival in the rap world, Tupac Shakur.

On September 7, 1996, Tupac was cruising as a passenger through the bright lights of Las Vegas. At 11:15 p.m., a white late-model Cadillac pulled up next to his vehicle, and an occupant wound down his window and pumped four shots into Shakur. One bullet entered the rapper's right lung. He was taken to the University Medical Center of Southern Nevada, and for six days doctors struggled to keep him alive. He was placed in an induced coma but the wounds were too severe, and on September 13 he died from respiratory failure and internal bleeding.

ABOVE **Originally, Tupac and Notorious B.I.G. collaborated in several musical ventures. They fell out, and both were gunned down by rival gangs.**

Soon after Tupac's death, the word went around that Notorious had played a role in the killing and supplied the gun to the attacker. The two had once been firm friends but had fallen out over gang connections. B.I.G. was affiliated with the Crips, and Tupac was a member of the Bloods. These violent street gangs are still the terror of L.A.

It seems Tupac might have provoked his own assassination. Earlier that night, he and his crew had set upon Orlando Anderson—one of the Crips' hardest men. This assault was caught on camera. Anderson was not one to take it lying down, and it is likely that his crew tracked the singer and shot him as payback. German Geco-brand bullets were used—the L.A. gangs' favorite slug.

Six months later, Notorious B.I.G. was called to L.A. to present at an awards ceremony. He was walking into the lion's den. Despite multiple death threats, he went out that fateful night to a party where many Crips and Bloods were present guarding rap industry figures.

While no one has been fingered for the assassination, it is likely that the Bloods decided on some payback. The bullets that slammed into Notorious B.I.G. were, you guessed it, 9mm Gecos.

Of course, the real question is—who was the best rapper? Tupac Amaru Shakur (aka Lesane Parish Crooks) has sold more than 75 million albums, while the Notorious B.I.G. (aka Christopher George Latore Wallace) has sold maybe 25 million.

Final Catwalk

Designing handbags, shoes, and frocks is not usually seen as a dangerous occupation. But fashion designer Gianni Versace made the fatal mistake of attracting the attention of a psychopathic homosexual murderer, who gunned him down in front of his own home.

There were many fashion crimes committed during the 1980s. However, Versace always managed to combine good taste with flamboyance. The fashionista was born of humble origins in Reggio Calabria, Italy, on December 2, 1946. His father was an electrical goods salesman, while his mother was a dressmaker. The young Versace obviously preferred frilly materials to toasters and learned the trade of designing and sewing at his mother's knee. By 1972 he was handling one-off commissions, and in 1978 he launched his first clothing range in Milan. By 1989 he was at the top of his trade, and his clothing empire catered to the elite. Princess Diana, Elton John, and Madonna all saw him as a personal friend. His assorted business interests were making the once-humble fashion designer tens of millions of dollars'

LEFT A Versace boutique in Milan. Gianni Versace founded his company in 1978 and was favored by the rich and powerful.

ABOVE Versace's South Beach mansion in Miami, USA. He was gunned down on the steps returning with the morning paper.

profit per annum. Even better: in the middle of 1997 he received the good news that his ear cancer was in remission, and his HIV test had come back negative.

This wondrous existence all came to a shocking end on July 15, 1997. On that morning, Versace had stepped out of his gorgeously decorated Italian-style villa on the Miami foreshore to get breakfast, the newspaper, and some magazines. As he returned from his shopping trip just before 9 a.m., a man stepped up behind him, pulled a pistol out of his backpack, and fired two shots into the back of the fashion designer's head. One of the shots shattered his lower jaw. As one witness described, he lay in a pool of blood "with his face blown off." He was rushed to Miami Memorial Hospital's Ryder Trauma Center, where he was pronounced dead at 9:15 a.m.

Witnesses described the killer as in his mid-twenties, dressed in a white shirt, dark shorts, and a white cap. The man walked away calmly, and soon afterward the pistol and the suspect's clothes were found in an abandoned pickup truck parked nearby. The police knew who they were looking for straight away. The male prostitute Andrew Cunanan had been on the FBI's most wanted list for several years.

Born on August 31, 1969, in National City, California, Cunanan soon proved to be a precocious individual at school. Eager to entertain with his rapid-fire wit, he covered an emptiness within by playing the fool. He was obviously camp, something that must have distressed his straitlaced Catholic mother and authoritarian Filipino father. Another thing noticed by his peers was Cunanan's almost continuous lying and storytelling. He was classified as having genius IQ and had a photographic memory. Soon he developed a sense of entitlement that the world owed him a lavish lifestyle.

ABOVE **Gianni Versace was a regular on the Miami gay scene. He may have had a passing encounter with his killer Cunanan.**

The handsome young man soon dropped out of school and by the age of 15 was a regular at the local gay bars. He began to earn a living as a rent boy; trading his vivacious good looks for hard cash from wealthy older gay men, he lived a fantasy life, spending all he could get on clothes, drugs, and sex. In his early twenties, a disturbing new character trait began to emerge: Cunanan acquired a taste for sado-masochistic sex.

The young gigolo relocated to San Francisco, where he pretended that he was a naval officer. He led the high life and in the gay community's frenzied social scene met many powerful individuals—including, briefly, Gianni Versace. A friend reported that in 1990 the fashion designer seemed to recognize Cunanan at the Colossus nightclub.

However, behind the smiling facade, a darker side to Cunanan's nature continued to develop. He acted in violent porn movies and began to drink excessively, alienating his clientele and scaring his friends. He began to obsess about AIDS and developed a paranoid persecution complex. At the same time, he maintained a lavish lifestyle through drug dealing.

Cunanan descended into madness. While there is no real motive for his killings, it seems he resented wealthy and powerful homosexuals and decided on getting some payback. His first victim was his successful ex-boyfriend, Jeff Trail, who had his skull stove in with multiple blows from a hammer during an argument with Cunanan and another ex-lover, David Madson. The latter, too, was murdered when Cunanan pulled a gun on him and shot him once in the head, once in the eye, and once in the back. Madson had probably been held hostage after witnessing Trail's murder.

The assassin then became a classic spree killer. While his first two victims had, in Cunanan's deranged imagination, deserved to die, his next victims were simply in the wrong place at the wrong time. Lee Miglin was standing outside his house when he was approached by Cunanan, asking for directions. The real estate tycoon was then bundled into his garage, where Cunanan perhaps played out his sadomasochistic fantasies to the full. He was known as a "dominator" in gay circles, and Miglin suffered a horrendous death. His hands and feet were bound, and his entire body was covered in tape, brown paper, and plastic. There were only two small holes for the older man to breathe out of his nostrils. Cunanan killed his victim slowly, first bashing him in the ribs, breaking several, then stabbing Miglin in the chest with some garden shears. How long the maniacal torture continued is not known, before he finished off his victim by sawing open his throat with a blunt bow saw, a horrific way to die.

The next victim was 45-year-old William Reese, who was held up and shot by the increasingly deranged killer. Cunanan stole Reese's red pickup truck and fled the scene, abandoning a Lexus he had stolen from Miglin.

Cunanan now had the fame he perhaps had dreamed of all his life. Notoriety would be a better word, and he ended up on the FBI's Ten Most Wanted list. Despite this, he moved to Miami and for two months hid in plain sight, leading a lifestyle of easy grace, living in a cheap hotel and dining in cafes and restaurants. While he was there he stalked Versace, noting his routine and working out the perfect time for an attack. Versace's early morning trip to the newsagent three blocks away seemed to be that perfect time.

After shooting Versace, Cunanan fled to a municipal car park and changed his clothes, standing next to the pickup truck he stole from Reese. Investigators soon found his abandoned clothes, along with the offender's passport and some pawn tickets.

RIGHT Andrew Cunanan was placed on the FBI's "Ten Most Wanted Fugitives" list.

He holed up in a mothballed luxury houseboat at a marina only 3 miles (5 kilometers) from the scene of the crime until July 25, when a janitor alerted authorities that he had heard somebody moving around inside the boat. A SWAT team surrounded the boat, ready for a shootout. It was not necessary. When, after a five-hour siege, they stormed on board under cover of tear gas and smoke grenades, they found Cunanan dead from a self-inflicted gunshot to the roof of his mouth.

An Unpleasant Precedent

While not a world changer, the assassination of Theo van Gogh on November 2, 2004, was the first time a high-profile murder by a Muslim fundamentalist sought to challenge Western democratic institutions such as free speech and religious tolerance.

Born in The Hague, Netherlands, on July 23, 1957, Van Gogh proved to be something of an abrasive character, who used his famous relative's notoriety (he was Vincent van Gogh's great-nephew) to carve out a media career of sorts. Involved in the stage, he also directed several films that often had a political theme.

He was particularly critical of Islamic fundamentalism and was alarmed by the influx of Muslims to Europe during the

BELOW **Theo van Gogh as a young man photographed in 1984. By 2004 he was overweight and an easy target for his assassin.**

1990s. He formed a creative alliance with Ayaan Hirsi Ali, a young Somalian woman who had fled an arranged marriage. The pair produced a short film, *Submission*, that highlighted the way in which some Islamist societies allow violence against women. Parts of the Koran were written in henna on the abused women's bodies, inflaming Muslim outrage against the artists. Van Gogh had always courted outrage and controversy but he did not expect the response he received.

As he cycled to work on the chilly morning of November 2, 2004, a Muslim assassin, the 26-year-old Mohammed Bouyeri, rode up to Van Gogh, dismounted, pulled out a Czech-made HS2000, and fired several bullets. Several hit Van Gogh, as well as some civilians passing by. Bouyeri continued to advance on his victim, who staggered away, pleading for mercy and gasping, "Please, no, please, no."

ABOVE **Even today, many years after Van Gogh's murder, Ayaan Hirsi Ali requires protection from a security detail due to the many threats made against her.**

Van Gogh's attacker was born in Amsterdam of Moroccan parents. His background echoed what is now a script but at the time shocked many in the Western world. Born into a moderate family, he had a troubled upbringing and sought solace in radical Islamic teaching. He wore a full djellaba, grew a beard, and attended mosques frequently, where he was exposed to radical Muslim orthodoxy calling for jihad.

His pent-up hate and frustration were taken out on Van Gogh. As the Dutchman stumbled away, Bouyeri pursued him to the curb and emptied his magazine into his victim's body. The assassin then pulled from his knapsack a large knife and slit Van Gogh's throat, almost decapitating the artist in the process. Bouyeri then thrust the knife, using his entire body weight, deep into Van Gogh's chest. Such was the violence of the wound that the knife penetrated through to the spinal column. The fanatical Muslim was still not finished with his demonstration, and he stuck a smaller knife into the Dutchman's chest, pinning verses from the Koran to the now dead body of his victim. The note also contained a death threat to Ayaan Hirsi Ali.

Bouyeri never had a chance to carry out that threat. Pursued by police, the killer was shot in the leg and arrested. On July 26, 2005, he was sentenced to life imprisonment with no chance of parole.

The murder sparked a wave of grief and outrage throughout Europe and the world. Sadly, attacks such as that committed by Bouyeri have become commonplace, and this event merely heralded the many atrocities perpetrated since.

Chapter 6
Mafia Hits

All individuals who decide to join the Mafia know that their chances of dying peacefully in bed are dramatically reduced by that decision. Violence is a way of life for these career criminals, and the most successful mob member is often the man who has the least tender feelings for his associates. Mafiosi don't only have to be on their guard from rival clans. As these hits show, most dead mafiosi are taken out by their nearest and dearest.

The Moe Greene Special

Bugsy Siegel is an icon of American gangster history. Portrayed in many movies, he is the inspiration for the character Moe Greene in *The Godfather*. This hoodlum is dispatched in a mafia hit now known as the "Moe Greene Special"—a revolver slug straight through the eyeball. This is only loosely based on Bugsy's assassination; he received several shots into the back of his head, one of which blew out the gangster's eyeball.

Benjamin Siegel was born into a Jewish migrant family on February 28, 1906. Raised in Brooklyn, his siblings grew up to be respectable members of the community, while Benjamin soon proved to be a handful for his despairing parents. He gained the nickname "Bugsy" thanks to his fiery violent temper, which could erupt for no reason.

He was attracted to lowlife hoodlums and even as a teenager ran protection rackets targeting poor peddlers. Another scam involved the young criminal driving taxis and taking well-heeled New Yorkers to the theater. While they were enjoying the show, Siegel and his gang would break into their residences and clear out any valuables. He had to drop this scheme when he was accused of raping a passenger and sacked.

BELOW **Meyer Lansky was the money man behind many casinos in Cuba and Las Vegas. A report that Siegel was skimming money was the last straw.**

Siegel hit the big league when he teamed up with another Jewish hoodlum, Meyer Lansky. The Bugsy–Meyer gang terrorized many New York boroughs and set up Murder Inc., a gang of desperate killers who were hired to carry out mob hits. Bugsy himself established a reputation as a stone-cold killer and was part of the team that took out many old-school mafiosi, including Sicilian mobster Joe "The Boss" Masseria in 1931.

Although not Italian, Siegel earned so much respect that he was invited by "Lucky" Luciano to set up the original National Crime Syndicate (see box on page 177) that ruled organized crime from the 1920s until today.

In 1937, Siegel relocated to California to set up new rackets and led an extravagant lifestyle in Beverly Hills. The original exponent of

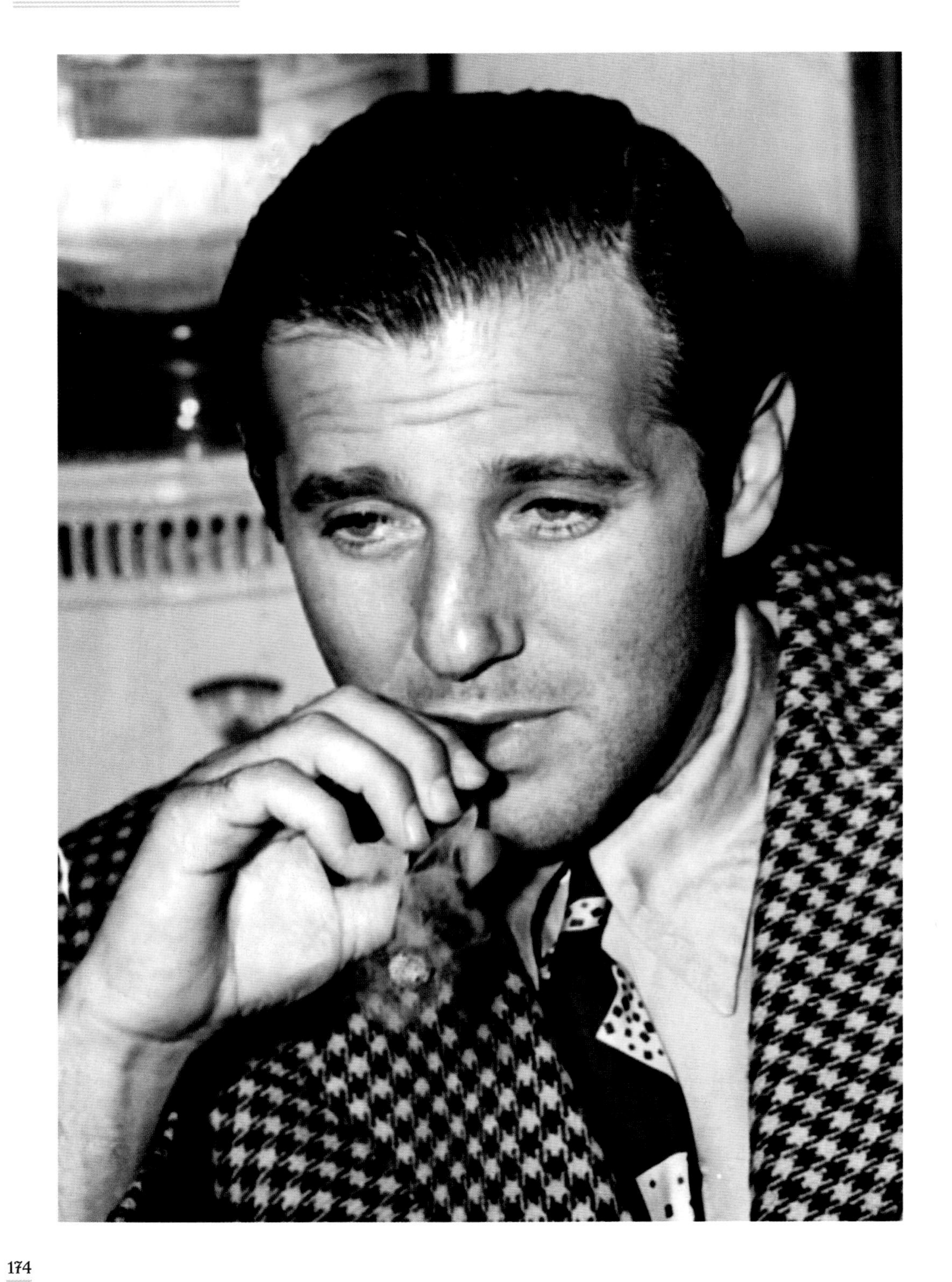

"gangster chic," he was at all the best parties and bedded a succession of starlets; but despite the gloss, his wealth was still based on violence and corruption. Offshore gambling ships, prostitution, narcotics, protection rackets, murder, and blackmail were Siegel's bread and butter.

He took control of the legal betting wire service, and it was while visiting one of his operatives that he came across a sleepy town called Las Vegas deep in the barrens of the Nevada desert. This was near a large army base and already had some smaller gambling establishments but Bugsy was determined to build a gambling mecca and borrowed funds from the Eastern syndicate to start building his dream: The Flamingo Hotel and Casino. It was named after his girlfriend's flaming red hair.

The original budget in 1945 was predicted to be 1.5 million dollars, but production costs soon soared to 6 million. Bugsy pleaded for more money to finish the project but it soon became clear he was skimming millions and mismanaging the whole project. Even when the casino finally opened, it lost millions of dollars due to some fortunate punters and bad luck for the house. The original casino did not have accommodation so big winners took their money elsewhere rather than staying overnight and blowing it when their luck turned. That, at least, is what Siegel told the East Coast Commission. Bugsy had skimmed the last of the cream as far as his mafiosi backers, including Lansky, were concerned. A hit was ordered.

Although he knew something was up, Siegel didn't take normal precautions for his safety. He often visited the mansion

LEFT **Benjamin "Bugsy" Siegel's Hollywood good looks concealed his violent temper and belief that violence solved many problems.**

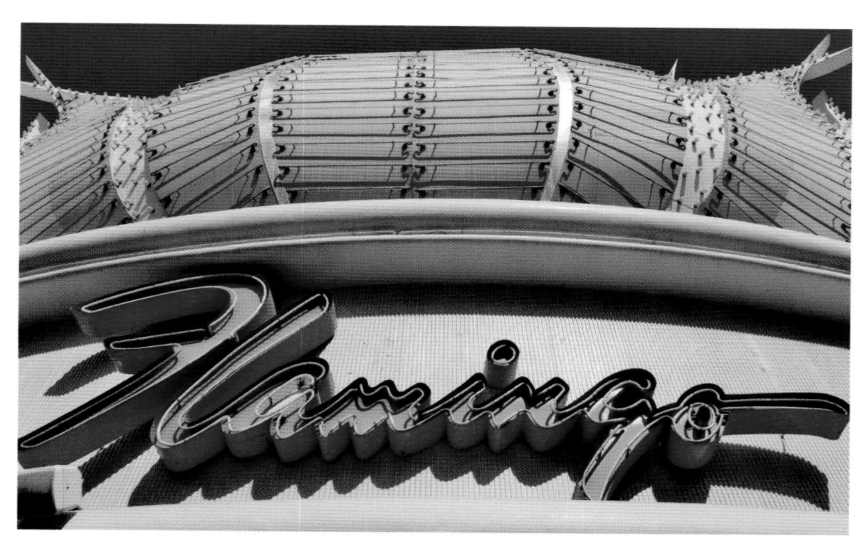

BELOW **The Flamingo Hotel and casino. A new management team moved in the day after Bugsy's assassination to turn it into a profitable venture.**

belonging to his girlfriend, Virginia Hill, and usually the blinds were drawn at nighttime. On the evening of June 20, 1947, this elementary precaution was not taken. This may indicate it was an inside job but, whatever the reason, it was catastrophic for the Jewish gangster.

At approximately 10:45 p.m., he was sitting on a floral couch with his back to the uncovered window, reading the *Los Angeles Times*. His assassin crept through the ornate flower beds and propped a .30 caliber military M1 carbine on the windowsill, aiming directly at the back of Bugsy's head. This was a handy high-velocity weapon with its semiautomatic function allowing for rapid fire. The assassin fired off half a magazine into the gangster's head. One bullet penetrated his right cheek and exited

BELOW **Siegel's body lies slain by gunfire on a couch in the house of girlfriend Virginia Hill.**

The Five Families

In the United States there are approximately 20 Mafia families, originally based on the East Coast. They are headed by the "Commission," whose decisions are binding on all the families. The current key families are the Gambinos (originally Mangano), Bonannos (Maranzano), Colombos (Profaci), Genovese (Luciano), and Lucchese (Gagliano). Also on the Commission is the Chicago outfit, whose most famous boss was Al Capone. Several of the main five families also represent minor Mafia families. The Commission was founded in 1931, and its first head was "Lucky" Luciano. The National Crime Syndicate, founded in 1929, was a loose coalition of organized crime gangs that were not solely Italian.

ABOVE **"Scarface" Capone is shown here at the Chicago Detective Bureau following his arrest on a vagrancy charge.**

through the left side of his neck. Another struck the bridge of his nose, blowing the left eye out of its socket. Part of his eyelid, with eyelashes still attached, was blown as far as the lounge door.

The killer made a quick exit, and the closest the police got to apprehending a suspect was the vague report of a black car that "headed north on North Linden toward Sunset Boulevard."

No gun or murderer was ever found. One theory named Chuck Hill, the brother of Siegel's girlfriend. He was an ex-marine and would have been familiar with the M1. Another theory was that the killer was Frankie Carbo, an old comrade from Murder Inc. who was tapped to rub out his ex-boss.

While the killer is not known, what is sure is that Bugsy's hit caused a media sensation, with pictures of his body splashed across all the nation's daily newspapers. The very next day, the other Mafia stakeholders moved straight into Siegel's casinos and took control, ensuring any profits went straight to the Eastern families.

Death at the Barbers

Albert Anastasia was a violent man. He was known as the "Mad Hatter" and "The Lord High Executioner." Anastasia was born in 1902 and emigrated from his Italian homeland in 1917, jumping ship in New York. He soon established a reputation for brutality and was nicknamed "the Mad Hatter" in recognition that those in this trade often went mad due to the mercury-based compounds they worked with. Anastasia had a hair-trigger temper and often ordered killings, or carried them out himself, on the spur of the moment. His early criminal career almost caught up with him, and he spent 1921 and 1922 on death row at Sing Sing prison, until he was released on a technicality.

Anastasia's ruthlessness saw him rise to the top of the Mafia hierarchy, and he was soon sitting on the Commission. During the 1930s, 40s, and 50s, Murder Inc. was responsible for the death of at least 1,000 people (see box on page 180).

However, by the 1950s the gloss was starting to wear off, and many top Mafia figures saw "The Lord High Executioner" as a wild card who was drawing too much heat onto the mob. Additionally, he was engaged in a turf war with the up-and-coming mob figure Vito Genovese while trying to muscle in on other Commission members' lucrative Cuban drug cartel. Perhaps what signed his death warrant was the fact that several times he had cleared out his crew with ruthless bloody purges, and many of even his closest confidants were wary of his violent nature.

These deadly pigeons came home to roost on the morning of Friday October 25, 1957, when Albert Anastasia went for his regular shave at the barber shop of New York's Park Sheraton Hotel. As usual, he strolled over to chair No. 4 and ordered "the works" from the obsequious barber, Joseph Bocchino. Anastasia didn't smell a rat when his bodyguard, Tony Coppola, took off for a cup of coffee across the road. He should have smelled two big rats armed with pistols coming his way.

As Anastasia reclined, Bocchino lathered his jaw with thick foamy shaving cream while placing steaming hot towels over the mob boss's eyes and forehead. Suddenly, everything went quiet when two masked gunmen entered the salon. They waved aside staff and customers before marching straight up to the prostrate Anastasia,

He tore off the hot towels, saw the guns pointing square at him, and struggled to get out of the chair, covering his face with his hands. The two assassins let loose, and five bullets smashed into his head and chest.

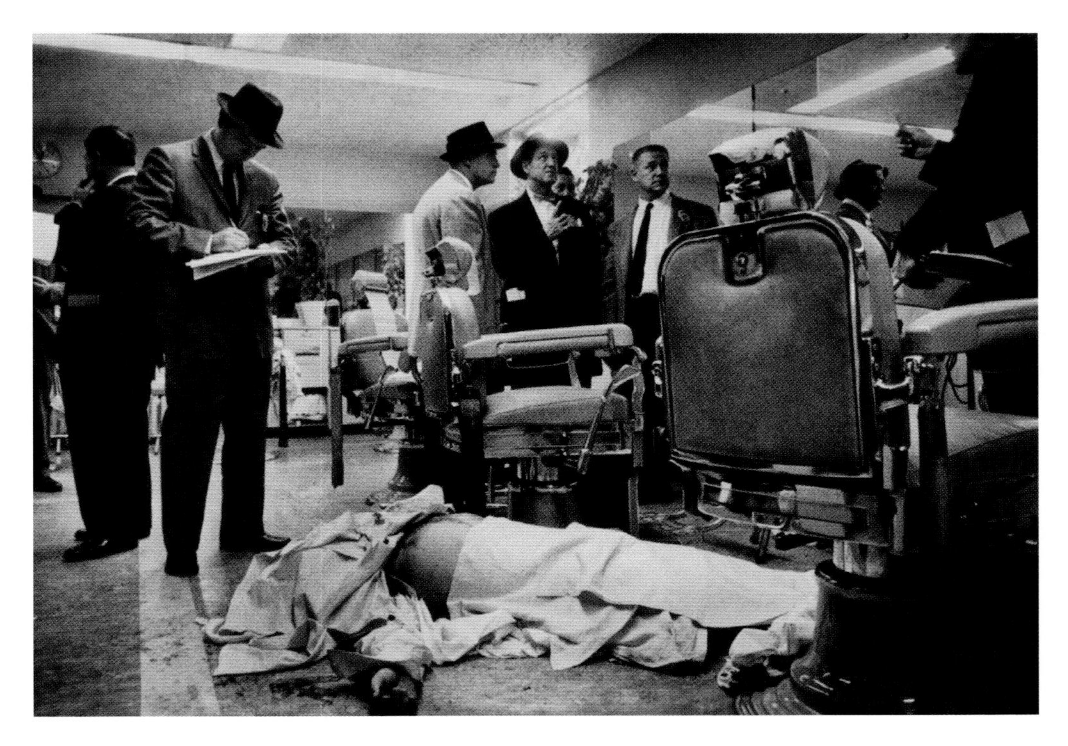

ABOVE **The body of Albert Anastasia. He gained a reputation as Brooklyn's toughest enforcer.**

leveling their firearms, a .32 and a .38, at their mark. Anastasia sensed something was wrong, but too late. He tore off the hot towels, saw the guns pointing square at him, and struggled to get out of the chair, covering his face with his hands. The two assassins let loose, and five bullets smashed into his head and chest. This wasn't enough to finish the job, and their victim managed to get out of the chair, lunging at one of the shooters before smashing into the mirrored barber's wall. He fell backward, crashing to the floor and taking any number of sweet-smelling lotions and colognes with him. The killers emptied their pistols into the prone body and, once the job was done, disappeared into the busy foot traffic of 7th Avenue.

All this time, Coppola was eating breakfast across the road. It's possible that not only was he told to clear out at the right time, but he was the inside guy who kept the hit team in the loop as to their mark's whereabouts.

Albert Anastasia's assassination was a classic Mafia hit. As a respected member, he was given no inkling of what was likely to occur; it happened almost in a split second. No civilians were hit, and, more importantly, even today nobody is sure who did the deed.

Murder Inc.

The Mafia in America first grabbed national headlines in the 1930s and 40s when they moved from small-time racketeers to become a well-organized machine with a team of dedicated hitmen, based in Brooklyn. Dubbed by the press as Murder Inc., these ruthless men gained a reputation as hard-handed killers. The methods they developed are still used today in high-profile assassinations. One of their chief leaders was Albert Anastasia (see page 178), who quickly gained a reputation as one of their most ruthless killers.

By the 1930s, the top Mafia families had formed the "Syndicate." This group sought to ensure that both their illicit and legal schemes were run in a businesslike manner. Territories were assigned and conflicts resolved. However, if a hit was called for, Murder Inc. would be given the job. They were dispatched right up and down the East Coast but also carried out assassinations in Florida, Detroit, and Los Angeles.

The methods used by the assassins were as varied as they were violent. The ice pick was a favorite weapon but offenders could be buried alive, thrown off buildings, strangled with a garrote, shot, buried in quicklime, and even vaporized with a car bomb. One individual was hogtied with a garrote around his neck so that any time he moved he choked himself. Prison was no safe place and Murder Inc. had operatives inside the joint who could substitute medicine with poison.

It was ensured that the killer wasn't personally acquainted with the target. Someone who knew the victim would take the assassination team to see what the victim looked like and then the hit team were to decide how best to carry out the execution. The target's habits and routines were ascertained and the site for the hit was chosen to minimize the chances of escape. Routes into and out of the site were meticulously worked out, with each member of the team given a role. Backup shooters were usually on hand. Several cars would be stolen a few weeks prior to the hit and given dummy plates. One was used for the killing party while a second was used as backup or to block any pursuers. Weapons were purchased, used, and then destroyed along with the stolen cars and, often, the body.

LEFT Louis "Lepke" Buchalter ran one arm of "Murder Inc." He escaped the assassin's bullet but died in the electric chair.

An Australian Hit

Griffith is a small town 373 miles (600 kilometers) west of Sydney, Australia. Stuck in the middle of the huge state of New South Wales, surrounded by semi-arable lands, it seems like the last place on earth to have a community of Mafia hoodlums. Not so. Many individuals have disappeared from their homes, never to be seen again. Disposed of in concrete pours or pigpens, those who have crossed the Mafia have met untimely and unpleasant ends. Rocco Medici and Giuseppe Furina's corpses were recovered in 1984. Whether this gave their family any closure is open to speculation. Both men had their hands tied behind their backs and their ears sliced off and were then shot between the eyes before being tossed into the Murrumbidgee River.

Griffith is a rich agricultural area due to an extensive irrigation scheme. Attracted to the area in the first half of the 20th century were many farmers from the Calabrian region in the "toe" of Italy. The warm weather was similar to their hometowns, and they brought many Italian traditions and crops with them. Some also brought their less savory aspects of Italian culture and were members of the secret Calabrian group the 'Ndràngheta—the honored society. This group began large-scale production of marijuana, and soon millions of dollars were pouring into the region. Supplying much of the East Coast of Australia with pot, the Mafia used their ill-gotten gains to build mansions, aptly named "grass castles," as well as buying off the local police and politicians.

Donald Mackay saw the consequences of the drug trade in his hometown and decided to do something about it. He was an aspiring politician and used his profile to rail against the insidious

BELOW **The view from Griffith Lookout. The bucolic pastoral scenes belie a history of violent organized crime in the area.**

nature of the drug trade. Many in the community sympathized with him and often gave him tip-offs while he sat in the local bar. The corrupt local police didn't act on Mackay's information so he took it to the Drug Squad commander in Sydney. This led to the biggest marijuana bust in Australian history. Tons of cannabis, an arsenal of weapons, and five members of the local Mafia were seized.

Inadvertently, the police released Mackay's name as the informer. This slip prompted the local kingpins, in particular the drug-dealing gambler Robert Trimbole, to arrange for the politician to be executed.

On July 15, 1977, Donald Mackay locked up his furniture store and drove his minivan to the Hotel Griffith to have a beer with his buddies. An hour later, he walked toward his car. As he reached into his pockets for the car keys, the gun for hire, James Frederick Bazley, stepped behind Mackay and planted three bullets in his brain. Bazley had the nickname "Mr. Cool", and his favorite weapon was a silenced .22. There were no witnesses, although a nearby office worker heard a couple of short sharp cracks and some groans. The victim dropped to the ground, spraying blood over his car door and onto an adjacent fence. Bazley bundled the campaigner's corpse into the boot of his own vehicle and drove off to dispose of the body. Traces of hair and skin were later found on the tarmac, as were the murdered man's keys, which fell under his car, and the handprint he left on the minivan's window as he staggered forward.

Bazley was paid 10,000 Australian dollars for the hit and instructed to make sure the body was never found. He stuck to his side of the bargain and despite a reward of $200,000 being posted for the recovery of Mackay's remains, they have never come to light. Some macabre theories have been hinted at, including the use of a sausage grinder and freshwater cray traps. Most likely Mackay is buried somewhere in the arid surrounds of Griffith.

Bazley was convicted for the crime but has never shown any remorse. He was also convicted for the contract murder of two drug mules, Isabel and Douglas Wilson, who were killed in 1979. Bazley was paid $20,000 for the double murder. He was also told to kill the Wilsons' dog, Taj. As a dog lover and former poodle breeder, he refused. The dog was later found wandering in a suburb of Melbourne.

INADVERTENTLY, THE POLICE RELEASED MACKAY'S NAME AS THE INFORMER. THIS SLIP PROMPTED THE LOCAL KINGPINS, IN PARTICULAR THE DRUG-DEALING GAMBLER ROBERT TRIMBOLE, TO ARRANGE FOR THE POLITICIAN TO BE EXECUTED.

The Last Lunch

As Carmine Galante turned up for lunch at his favorite family-run restaurant, he appeared to all the world like a kindly Italian grandfather. Informally dressed, and with a relaxed air, the bald and bespectacled 69-year-old sat down in the picturesque courtyard and ordered his favorite pasta, just like thousands of other Italians worldwide. However, this lunch, on July 12, 1979, was to be his last.

Appearances are deceptive. Galante was a Mafia boss who funneled the proceeds of a huge narcotic empire, stretching from Sicily to America, through his criminal empire, and was responsible for at least 60 hits. He had many nicknames; chief among them was "Cigar Galante," as he always seemed to have a cigar in his mouth, whether he was at a family get-together or ordering a hit.

He was born in Harlem on February 21, 1910 and soon proved to be a troublesome youth. As early as the age of 10 he had been arrested for minor criminal acts, and by 15 he had formed his own street gang. At the age of 16 he was convicted of assault and sentenced to two-and-a-half years' imprisonment.

He then spent nearly the whole 1930s behind bars for shooting a police officer, only emerging well into 1939. While in custody, he underwent a battery of psychological tests and was found to have psychotic tendencies, along with a subnormal IQ of 80; but Galante made up for this lack of intelligence with plenty of rat-like cunning. On release, he became an enforcer for the Luciano family and during this period may have had a hand in 80 murders. He then joined the Bonanno family and became an underboss. While working for Joe Bonanno, he learned the ropes of the family heroin business. In 1957, Galante pioneered a new scheme where the Sicilian Mafia brought the drugs to America, while the Bonannos were in charge of distribution. Along with the heroin came "zips," tough Sicilian mob members who were used as assassins in the USA for short periods before heading home. They also acted as bodyguards and were intensely loyal due to their lack of English and their dependence on the boss.

In July 1962, Galante was locked up for 20 years on a narcotics charge. After serving for 12 years, the hardened and ruthless mob boss was released and found that his operation had been largely taken over by the Gambino family. He soon took back control by ordering the hits

BELOW Carmine Galante. As a young man he was sentenced to 20 years. Upon release he took on the powerful mafia families.

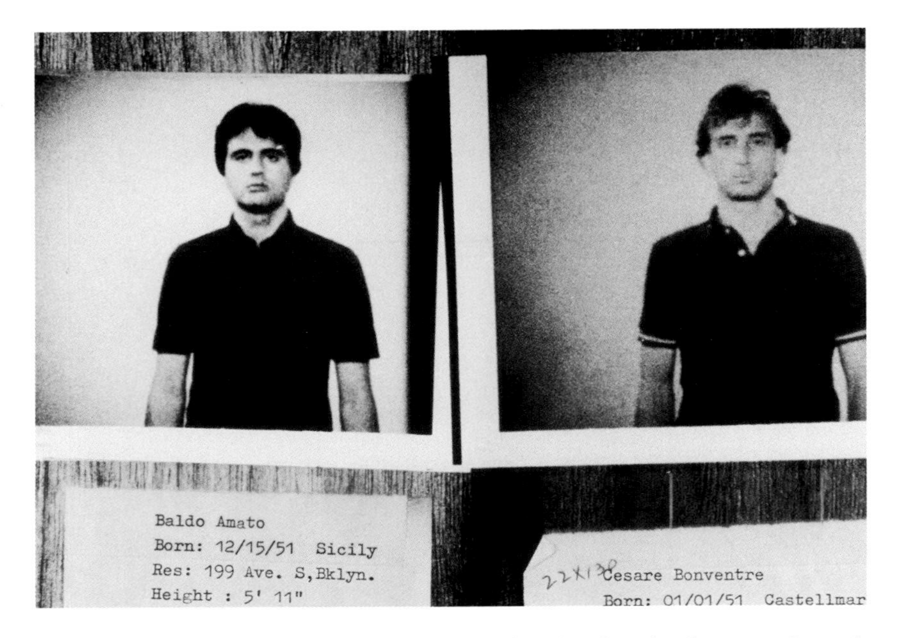

ABOVE **The Sicilian "zips" Baldo Amato (left) and his cousin Cesare "The Tall Guy" Bonventre (right).**

of at least eight top Gambinos. The other four families were alarmed. They were also upset that the Bonanno boss wasn't sharing the proceeds of his lucrative operation. In 1979, the Commission decided Galante had reached his use-by date.

Galante was fearless and threatened even more top-level hits against other families. This was partly because he believed his zips were loyal and always looking after his back. On July 12, 1979, he had two zips as his bodyguards. Baldo Amato and Cesare Bonventre stood out on that sweltering summer day—while all those around them wore light trousers and short-sleeved shirts, the two Sicilians wore leather jackets. Each was carrying a small arsenal of handguns, as is customary with Mafia bodyguards. These two hired guns were cousins and came from Galante's parents' hometown, Castellammare del Golfo on the northwest tip of Sicily.

Experienced mafiosi who suspect they are in danger ensure that they vary their routine. Galante obviously had no such anxieties, as he turned up at the regular time for his midday meal at "Joe and Mary's Italian–American Restaurant" at 205 Knickerbocker Avenue, Brooklyn. As usual combining business with pleasure, Galante was there to meet the owners of the restaurant, Giuseppe Turano and Leonard Coppola. Turano was a Bonanno soldier who made his profits by selling contraband meat, while Coppola was a Bonanno capo. The two had had a falling out over Turano's wife, and Galante had summoned them to reach a settlement and make peace. While Turano's son and mother prepared food within the restaurant, the three mobsters, along with Amato and Bonventre, sat outdoors on the patio.

Knickerbocker Avenue was the heartland of the Bonanno crime family and Galante felt secure surrounded by killers who would do anything to enforce his rule. As he settled in the quaint courtyard, festooned with tomato vines, at the rear of the restaurant, he poured himself a glass of red wine and got stuck in to the seafood antipasto laid out by Turano.

At 2:40 p.m., just as the temperature peaked on that stifling hot day, a blue Mercury Montego (which had been stolen a month earlier) pulled up outside the restaurant. The driver, who was armed with an M1 carbine, stepped out of the vehicle and stood guard. Three others, their faces concealed, tumbled out of the vehicle and raced into "Joe and Mary's." The first gunman, carrying a pump-action shotgun, was followed by the second assassin, armed with a double-barreled shotgun. Bringing up the rear was a short, potbellied mobster armed with a pistol. Turano's son realized the danger and yelled a warning while running for a revolver in the storeroom. The third gunman forced open the storeroom door and put two bullets into the young man's back, effectively neutralizing any threat from the rear.

Galante and Turano heard the commotion and stood to meet any threat. Too late. The man armed with the double-barreled shotgun stepped into the courtyard and loosed both barrels into the startled

BELOW **The body of Carmine Galante lies in the courtyard of his favorite restaurant, Joe and Mary's.**

mob boss. As Galante pitched backward, he received another discharge from the double barrel into his back.

Turano screamed at the shooters before the pump-action shotgun was forced against his chest and discharged, blowing him off his feet as the shot went through his lungs, severing his carotid artery and blowing away part of his right shoulder and face. As Turano crashed to the ground, the shooter followed up with another three rounds, destroying his victim's right arm and blowing out his left eye.

Nor was Coppola going to escape. It's possible that one of the zips, Bonventre, pulled out a .30 caliber automatic handgun from his bulky leather jacket and fired five shots into the capo's face and chest. It seems the zip had an ax to grind—he emptied his magazine into Galante's lifeless corpse.

The shooter with the repeating shotgun then finished the job, using a couple of shells to blow off the top of Coppola's head. His brains were splattered all over the tomato vines and the restaurant wall. Seconds later, eyewitnesses saw the three ski-masked killers jump into the car. As it sped off down Knickerbocker Avenue, the two Sicilians, Bonventre walking stiffly with the handgun at his side, also left and were driven away in a blue Lincoln.

Turano's son survived the shooting. A classic mob hit had gone down. The shooters were never identified, no one was convicted for the crimes, the car and weapons were destroyed, a clean escape was made, and a dangerous mob boss who wasn't following Commission protocols was taken down. What's more, one of the shooters found the time to stick a cigar into the dead boss's mouth and a Zippo lighter into his stiffening right hand. "Cigar Galante's" dead body became an icon of Mafia hits.

Winter Shoot-out

Paul Castellano didn't attend the funeral of his mob protector, Neil Dellacroce. This was a bad call and led to "Big Paul's" own death—one of the smoothest hits in mob history.

Constantino Paul Castellano was born in Brooklyn to immigrant Sicilian parents on June 26, 1915. Deciding that hard work wasn't for him, he dropped out of school at about 14 years of age, worked in his father's butcher shop, and ran errands for the local mob-controlled bookmakers. When the young crook was arrested in 1934 for armed robbery, he was sentenced to three months but didn't "sing" to the police about who his two accomplices were. This ensured that the local mobsters thought he was "solid."

In 1937, he married into the Gambino crime family, one of the major Mafia pillars in New York. Paul developed many rackets involving bootlegging, illegal gambling, union infiltration, and rigging construction bids. The latter two sound harmless

enough, but many mob figures used union membership accounts as their personal piggy banks. Honest construction companies found that once they had given a contract to a Mafia-owned crane or building company, they were made an offer that it was unwise to reject for all subsequent projects. Non-Mafia contractors learned pretty quickly not to undercut quotes from the mob or they would be run out of town. Castellano's most profitable business was pouring concrete. He and several other mob-controlled concrete providers ensured that any jobs over two million dollars were handled by the cartel named "the Concrete Club." The Mafia-controlled Teamsters Union prevented any other work from going ahead.

When Carlo, the head of the Gambino family, died in 1976, Castellano was made head of the family and kept a low profile while ruling with an iron hand from his Staten Island mansion. Built to resemble the White House, it contained an Olympic-sized swimming pool and an English-style box hedge garden. He conducted most of his business here, and when the underbosses visited him, he held court in his luxurious silk dressing gown and slippers. This mansion proved to be his undoing, and in 1983 the federal authorities succeeded in planting a wiretap in the crime boss' kitchen. At the time, Castellano was having an affair with the maid, and an eavesdropping agent heard him get up to all kinds of mischief, including 600 hours of discussions about "family

ABOVE **Paul Castellano (center) made several key mistakes. He fell for an FBI bugging sting and kept to a regular routine dining at his favorite restaurant.**

BELOW **Carlo Gambino. When he named Paul Castellano as his successor, many of his subordinates resented the decision.**

business." This included the head of the family ordering up to 26 hits. He was arrested in March 1984 but released on a two-million-dollar bond. He was arrested a year later, along with other family bosses, during an investigation into mob control of construction in the Big Apple.

Released again, Castellano was also having trouble keeping his capos and made men in line. Due to several inexcusable blunders, he had brought both state and federal heat down on the Gambino family. Only Neil Dellacroce, one of Paul's trusted lieutenants, kept his men in line. In 1985, Dellacroce died, and Gambino couldn't be bothered with attending the wake. This was the last straw and John Gotti, later known as the "Teflon Don," made his move.

Castellano made a fatal error. Like Carmine Galante (see page 183), he, too, had a favorite eatery, Sparks Steak House, an upscale restaurant on 46th Street. Gotti knew it and set up a coordinated hit at Big Paul's usual chow time. Four shooters were detailed for the assassination, and, given the wintry conditions in downtown New York, they wore a "uniform" of sorts—a long white winter raincoat with deep pockets. Perfect for concealing a handgun. The touch of genius was that each man was also wearing a big Russian-style fur hat, common for New Yorkers on a cold day but also an excellent recognition symbol so each man

BELOW **Paul Castellano (on sidewalk) and his bodyguard Thomas Bilotti fell to an extremely well-choreographed hit with several shooters at Sparks Steak House.**

on the team could pick out his compatriots on the busy sidewalk. Each had a walkie-talkie, which allowed the hit to be coordinated to within a second's precision.

Gotti had set up the hit, and on Monday December 16, 1985, he was parked a short distance from Sparks Steak House, ready to watch it go down. His Lincoln town car was driven by one of the coldest killers in the family, Sammy "Bull" Gravano. As Castellano's bodyguard and driver, Thomas Bilotti, pulled to a stop in front of the popular eatery at 5:45 p.m., the team covered all points of the compass around the car, ready to take part. Castellano stepped out, and three men, all with the distinctive fur hats, converged on their target, unleashing a hail of bullets on the unarmed mob boss. Castellano fell to the frozen tarmac with six bullets in his head and chest, while Bilotti took four. One shooter stood over the target and pumped one more slug into his head, just to make sure. The once busy sidewalk had almost miraculously emptied, and the three gunmen were able to take off unimpeded. There were others in the team, all similarly dressed, acting as lookouts and backup in case something went wrong. Not required, they too faded into the background and made their way to a rendezvous at 2nd Avenue, where they were picked up in cars with stolen number plates.

As the killers scattered, Gotti drove slowly past his enemy, checked the result, and drove on. A hit that had taken four months to plan had gone remarkably smoothly. No civilians or police were involved, and Gotti's coup saw him installed as the boss of the Gambino family.

Motorway Blast

Giovanni Falcone was a spectacularly successful magistrate charged with clearing the mafiosi out of Sicily. He paid for it with his life. As Falcone, his wife, and several bodyguards were driving to Palermo airport, a half-ton bomb placed in an underpass was detonated under the motorcade. All the passengers died instantaneously, and the shock waves were registered on local earthquake monitors.

The Mafia ruled the roost in Sicily. Most judges, magistrates, and politicians were in the pockets of the Mafia. Extortion and corruption were rampant, leading to a breakdown of many civil services and the near collapse of law and order. Two dominant Mafia families were the Inzerillo and Spatola clans. They had links with the Gambino family in New York and moved tremendous quantities of heroin across the Atlantic. Falcone was placed in charge of investigating the operation, and in May 1980 Judge Gaetano Costa signed 53 arrest warrants against the two clans. They were not about to take this lying down, and he was gunned down in August 1980. Rome sent a general of the Italian elite Carabinieri to help with the anti-Mafia crackdown. He too was killed, with his young wife by his side. This was too much for the locals, and throughout Sicily the population rose up in anger, rioting and attacking politicians who they thought were soft on the Mafia. Rome had to act, and they gave Falcone extra powers to crack down on the local crime lords.

He used his new powers and tracked down million-dollar transactions. Acting as chief prosecutor, Falcone led a two-year trial that saw 360 mafiosi put away for lengthy stints. One of the most important factors in the trial was the testimony of Tommaso Buscetta, one of the first ever Sicilian mafiosi to become an informant (*pentito*). He was on the witness stand for an entire week. It was Falcone to whom Buscetta preferred to speak when revealing the secrets of the Mafia, and Buscetta later claimed that while other magistrates and detectives patronized him, Falcone treated him with respect.

Buscetta warned Falcone that the Mafia would come after him. This proved correct when in June 1989 a sports bag was found adjacent to Falcone's beach house. An alert guard found it but fortunately did not pick it up. It contained 58 sticks of plastic explosives, primed to explode if disturbed. It didn't explode—but the next attempt was spectacularly effective.

On May 23, 1992, on the orders of Salvatore "Totò" Riina, 500 kilograms of explosive was placed under the motorway between Palermo International Airport and the city of Palermo. Riina was the top boss of all the Sicilian families, and he wanted the execution to be as public as possible.

Giovanni Brusca was tasked with killing Falcone. It was he who selected the place of execution and ordered the explosives to be laid in a culvert under the motorway. Numerous tests were carried out to see if the explosives were powerful enough, and fake concrete culverts were blown up beforehand.

Once everything was set up, Brusca had the explosives laid and waited in a small outbuilding on a hill to one side of the motorway. As Falcone drove to the airport on that fateful day, Brusca detonated the charge. The blast was spectacularly successful, creating a 100-foot (30-meter) wide crater, vaporizing the front end of Falcone's car, and killing all its inhabitants with the shock wave. Other innocents were killed in the carnage. Riina threw a party and toasted Falcone's death with champagne. All of Italy was outraged and the net soon closed around the perpetrators.

Brusca was informed upon by a former associate, Giuseppe di Matteo. In an attempt to silence him, Brusca kidnapped Di Matteo's 11-year-old son and tortured him repeatedly, then sent photos of the torture to Di Matteo in order to get him to withdraw the damning testimony. The young boy did not survive the ordeal. He was finally strangled with a garrote, and his body was dissolved in a vat of acid. With good reason, Brusca had the nickname *lo scannacristiani* (the people slayer), but this did not help him, and both he and Riina were given life sentences.

RIGHT **Half a ton of high explosives was packed into a culvert waiting for Falcone's convoy to drive over it.**

PALERMO
CAPACI
Croma
ROMA RM OE4837

CHAPTER 7
NEAR MISSES

ASSASSINATIONS CAN CHANGE HISTORY. Within the blink of an eye, a stable government can be replaced by chaos, disunity, and civil war. Hindsight shows us that botched assassinations can be equally important. What would the world be like if Adolf Hitler had died in 1933? Would Eastern Europe still be dominated by the USSR if Ronald Reagan had died in 1981? One can only speculate how history would have turned out if bullets had been an inch to the left or bombs were detonated 20 minutes earlier.

A Very Curious Plot

Queen Elizabeth I and her diabolically cunning minister and chief of security, Sir Francis Walsingham, were engaged in a dastardly plot—to assassinate Queen Elizabeth I!

Or so it seemed. Elizabeth's rule (1558–1603) is now seen as a golden age in British history. During this time, England established herself on the world stage, and the foundations for her empire and navy were laid. It was a time of relative peace and prosperity, but most importantly a time of ordered and strong rule from Britain's

BELOW Queen Elizabeth I. She survived plots sponsored by the French, the Spanish, and the Scots.

monarch. But there was a thorn in Elizabeth's side. She could never truly rest securely on her throne while the pretender, Mary, Queen of Scots, lurked as an ever-present threat to her rule.

Henry VIII (1491–1547) had split from the Catholic Church in order to be able to marry Anne Boleyn, Elizabeth's mother. This had led to much conflict as Protestants loyal to the king attacked Catholics loyal to the pope. When Mary Tudor (1516–1558), a staunch Catholic, acceded to the throne after the brief reign of her Protestant half-brother, Edward VI (1537–1553), she earned the epithet "Bloody Mary" from her delight in burning Protestants. When Elizabeth ascended the throne on November 17, 1558, she declared herself to be a Protestant queen and sought to stop religious strife.

But Catholics within England and in Europe weren't satisfied—they wanted to return England to the papacy, and their best chance to do that lay with Mary, Queen of Scots. Born in 1542, she was the daughter of James V of Scotland and great-granddaughter of England's Henry VII, and her aim was to rule, as rightful heir, both Scotland and England. But even ruling Scotland was beyond her, and she was deposed and imprisoned in Loch Leven Castle in 1567. Soon she was in the custody of Elizabeth.

RIGHT **Elizabeth learned to rely on the judgment of her spymaster Sir Francis Walsingham. He tricked Mary Queen of Scots to reveal a deadly plot.**

ABOVE **Henry VIII's decision to split from the Catholic Church led to generations of sectarian conflict that threatened to bring down the Tudor dynasty.**

Nevertheless, she continued to cause trouble. Like a deadly ring around England, Catholic leaders, including the pope, were always conspiring to free Mary and depose Elizabeth. Walsingham saw that the situation could not continue. He cunningly installed some of his undercover operatives in Mary's household and facilitated a new plot to release Mary and depose Elizabeth. It is likely that Elizabeth gave at least tacit approval to her spymaster's involvement in what became known as the Babington Plot.

Walsingham's plans came to fruition when Mary, lulled into a false sense of security, wrote a coded letter in July 1586 agreeing to the plot to assassinate her cousin. Walsingham had the evidence he needed, and soon Mary was condemned to death.

On February 8, 1587, Mary was beheaded. It was, apparently, a botched job. The axman fluffed his lines, and it took two or three attempts to finally separate her head from her neck. To make things worse, as he picked up the head, he was left holding her wig while the head rolled off the scaffold!

Elizabeth's rule was now secure, and she had *not* succeeded in assassinating herself!

McNaughton Rule

An assassination attempt on the British prime minister Sir Robert Peel in 1843 may not have had world-shattering consequences, but it did lead to the McNaughton Rule—the first formalized attempt to deal with the insane in the courtroom.

On January 20, 1843, a Scotsman named Daniel McNaughton was determined to kill the prime minister Sir Robert Peel. McNaughton was suffering paranoid delusions and was sure that the government was persecuting him. His eyes fastened upon the prime minister's private secretary, Edward Drummond, as he was walking toward Downing Street. Certain that he had his man, McNaughton walked up to him, drew a pistol, and shot the civil servant in the back. He went to draw another pistol but was overpowered by a policeman.

At first it appeared that Drummond would survive when the ball was removed from his back. Five days later he succumbed to his injury and McNaughton was put on trial for murder. Both prosecution and defense agreed that McNaughton was unbalanced. He spoke of continually being shadowed and harassed by agents of the government who were clearly out to hound him to his grave. The defense, led by Alexander Cockburn, successfully argued that their client was not responsible for his actions due to reasons of insanity, and the accused Scotsman was acquitted.

LEFT This engraving of Daniel McNaughton from the *Illustrated London News*, 1843, does little to reveal his disturbed state of mind.

There was a need to clarify the verdict due to a storm of opposition and the English Chief Justices delivered a ruling in the House of Lords supporting the decision. Part of the ruling became the McNaughton Rule, which stated that to be acquitted on the grounds of insanity, the accused must be acting under such strong delusions that they do not know what they are doing, and if they do know what they are doing, that they do not know their actions are wrong.

These rules were adopted in the USA in 1849 and were used throughout the Commonwealth for at least 100 years. Jurisdictions now use the term "diminished responsibility" to determine the effect mental illnesses may have on murderous actions.

The Elusive Führer

Historians have identified more than 40 plans to assassinate Adolf Hitler. Most of these never got off the drawing board or were unrealistic. Maybe ten attempts got close to killing Hitler but only three posed a real danger to his life. The first was undertaken by the talented loner Georg Elser. Had he succeeded in his quest, Hitler would have been killed well before many of his murderous policies were put into place.

Hitler built a career on demonizing Jews, Communists, and the "November Criminals" who signed the ceasefire that ended World War I on November 11, 1918. He was convinced that all of these

BELOW Adolf Hitler's fleet of specially built Mercedes-Benz had many security features, including bulletproof tires.

groups were part of a vast conspiracy to destroy Germany and the Aryan race. However, it wasn't one of these "enemies" of Germany that almost brought Hitler's career to a premature end but a German citizen determined to right the wrong he saw all around him in the new Nazi state. Acting alone and displaying considerable cunning, Georg Elser came the closest to killing Hitler and preventing the apocalypse that overtook Germany and Europe in World War II.

Elser seemingly had three passions in life: hearty Bavarian food, good German beer, and killing Hitler. He was able to satisfy the first two desires and almost attained the third. Although loosely involved with the German Communist Party, his real hatred for Hitler seems to have developed due to a loathing of the dictator's bullying speeches and violent policies. These mirrored Elser's home life. He had been frequently beaten by his abusive father and seems to have transferred the anger caused by his upbringing on to Hitler.

In 1938, the trained watchmaker and craftsman visited the Munich Beer Hall, where he observed the Nazi festivities commemorating the abortive Beer Hall Putsch of 1923. This was Hitler's first attempt to seize power, and for many years he had given a commemoration speech at the same time, 9 p.m. on November 8. Elser determined that this would be the perfect time to do away with the tyrant and he determined to strike at that hour during the 1939 festivities. He decided to install his bomb in the large pillar just behind the dais upon which Hitler was to speak to the old comrades of the Beer Hall Putsch. The pillar also supported a gallery above the main beer hall, so not only would the detonation kill anybody nearby, but it would bring down the large gallery, squashing any who had the misfortune to be below.

Elser had a year to prepare and used this time to source dynamite and detonators as well as building an ingenious timing mechanism to set off his bomb. Once he had done this, he had to place the lethal device in the pillar. This was no small undertaking—the pillar was solid brick and stone, and required months of hammer and chisel work. It was covered with a veneer of timber, and Elser had to remove a panel so that he could work behind it while leaving no traces of sawdust or stone, lest his nefarious activities be detected.

For several months Elser would turn up at the Munich Bierkeller where Hitler had launched his Putsch in 1923. After dining on a crispy schnitzel jaeger (hunter's pork cutlet) or perhaps some Leberkäse (meatloaf) and downing a couple of steins of quality ale, he would disappear upstairs and hide in a storeroom until the bar staff locked up and went home for the evening. The clockmaker then snuck out of his hidey-hole and proceeded to install his bomb in the large pillar. The cavernous beer hall magnified any loud noises, meaning that he could only strike his chisel or make a loud noise when a train roared past or the automatic toilet-flushing

RIGHT **Hitler speaking at a reunion of Nazi Brownshirts at the Munich Beer Hall. He left minutes before a bomb was detonated.**

mechanism went off. Over several months, he was able to install the bomb; but the many hours spent kneeling took a toll on him physically. Despite wearing kneepads, his knees were reduced to suppurating wounds.

Finally, after many months, the bomb was ready. Elser installed it in its chamber and set the timer to detonate at the appointed time of Hitler's speech. He then headed for the German–Swiss border, confident that his bomb would kill the Führer.

The bomb worked perfectly. At 9:20 p.m. on the dot, the Bürgerbraükeller's main hall was shattered by a devastating explosion. Shattered timber and stone flew in all directions, cutting through flesh and breaking bones. The large gallery and part of the ceiling collapsed, while Hitler's dais was reduced to tinder.

One problem: Hitler was not there. Due to pressures brought about by the war situation, he had considered canceling his appearance, but instead came to a compromise with the organizers and began speaking earlier than scheduled, at 8 p.m. He left at 9:07 p.m. and when the bomb went off, only a few cronies and bar staff were still in the hall. Hitler had escaped, and became further convinced of his role as a man of destiny.

Things did not go smoothly for Elser at the German–Swiss border. Invited into the barracks for a chat by the border guards, he was rapidly implicated in the attempt by the contents of his pockets.

BELOW **The Burgerbraukeller beer hall after Elser's bomb exploded. The upper balcony fell where Hitler had been speaking minutes earlier.**

These included a fuse, some Communist propaganda, maps of Munich, a drawing of the beer hall, and, unbelievably, diagrams of his bomb. The would-be assassin was given over to the tender mercies of the Gestapo, who left no stone unturned to prove that he was part of a larger conspiracy.

ABOVE **Elser was questioned by the Gestapo long after his assassination attempt. Himmler refused to believe it was a lone-wolf attack.**

Elser was beaten, kicked (by no other than an enraged Himmler, whose security network he had so flagrantly breached), starved, and even hypnotized in attempts to get him to "roll over" and name his accomplices. Another bizarre Gestapo method was used to get him to spill the beans. He was placed in a small room with several heaters turned up to full blast. Elser was then force-fed salted herrings while being denied water or liquid of any kind. The ensuing rabid thirst was meant to force a confession.

But Elser could not confess, as he had worked alone. He spent several years in a concentration camp before being executed when the Nazis were tying up loose ends toward the end of the war. Himmler was particularly angry at this breach of security, as he had assumed responsibility for safeguarding Hitler.

The second attempt that came close to killing Hitler was the conspiracy of top German officers who penetrated his formidable array of military security. The officers

ABOVE **Henning von Tresckow, one of the key conspirators in a 1943 plan to blow Adolf Hitler's Condor out of the sky.**

of Army Group Centre had seen Hitler interfere with the Wehrmacht's drive on Moscow in 1941 and well knew the consequences of this disastrous order. As the once unstoppable German military became bogged down in the ruthless war of attrition on the Eastern Front, a coterie of conspirators decided that Hitler had to die.

The leader of this group was Colonel Henning von Tresckow. A decorated hero of World War I, he was also Field Marshal Fedor von Bock's nephew and had seen at first hand how Hitler had stymied his uncle's drive on Moscow. He was also disgusted by the crimes of the Einsatzgruppen (Nazi killing units) in Poland and Russia, and was horrified by the Führer directives that almost exhorted the armed forces to commit horrendous war crimes. Tresckow was Chief of Staff at Army Group Centre and used this positon to recruit other soldiers determined to bring down the Nazi regime, including his cousin Fabian von Schlabrendorff. The conspirators hatched various plans that included kidnapping and shooting Hitler, but finally determined that the best method would be to blow him out of the sky using captured British plastic explosive. Hitler was due to visit the headquarters of Army Group Centre, and that gave the conspirators the perfect opportunity to carry out their plan.

The two spent their off hours experimenting with different types of explosives and fuses and finally determined that the British explosive was the best choice. It was parachuted to resistance groups in large amounts. It had the benefits of being compact and powerful. Tresckow molded this deadly material into a package that looked like two bottles of Cointreau. He inserted a 30-minute fuse into the lethal device and just as Hitler and his entourage were about to depart on the morning of March 13, 1943, Tresckow asked Colonel Brandt, a member of Hitler's staff, if he could take the two bottles of brandy to a mutual friend. Breaching all security protocols, Brandt agreed,

THE CONSPIRATORS HATCHED VARIOUS PLANS THAT INCLUDED KIDNAPPING AND SHOOTING HITLER, BUT FINALLY DETERMINED THAT THE BEST METHOD WOULD BE TO BLOW HIM OUT OF THE SKY USING CAPTURED BRITISH PLASTIC EXPLOSIVE.

Wolf's Lair

Hitler's security detail was never tighter than at his various secure Führer Headquarters. The most famous installation was Wolf's Lair near Rastenburg in East Prussia (now Ketrzyn, Poland). Hitler spent more than two years in this vast complex. Located in the sparsely populated wooded district of Masuria, it had easy access by rail to Berlin and was virtually invisible from the air. Added to the natural camouflage provided by the local pine forests were extensive camouflage nets covering the bunkers and installations. These included aircraft hangars, barracks, a weather station, and a sauna. Up to 40 feet (12 meters) in height and with concrete foundations up to 23 feet (7 meters) deep, they would probably have been able to resist a blockbuster concrete penetration bomb. The 1.9 square mile (5 square kilometer) site was divided into three concentric circles of security. Each zone was delineated by barbed wire entanglements, bunkers, anti-tank gun positions, watchtowers, machine gun nests, and checkpoints. These formidable defenses were manned by nearly 2,000 soldiers sworn to protect Hitler. Passes were required to get into any of the zones, and the most difficult to gain access to was the inner security zone. Only about 60 of the fortress personnel were allowed in the inner sanctum of the Nazi empire, and they went through the most rigorous vetting. Any individual found within the concentric fortifications without the correct security would be shot on sight.

RIGHT **"Wolf's Lair" was Hitler's main secret headquarters in Poland. It was here that he saw his army's fortunes collapse on the Eastern Front.**

ABOVE **Hitler proclaimed that his survival after Colonel von Stauffenberg's attempt on his life was a miracle. He exacted a bloody revenge on the conspirators.**

and as the huge Condor rose into the sky the conspirators thought that "Operation Flash" would succeed.

For two hours they waited for news of a crash but were shocked to be informed that the plane had landed safely at Rastenburg. Shlabrendorff made a beeline to the Wolf's Lair (see box on page 203) and recovered the package from his trusting friend. Warily taking apart the bomb, he found that poor British workmanship had foiled the attempt. A faulty fuse had spared Hitler and removed the last chance for Germany to seek an honorable peace before the Allied armies closed in on the Fatherland. In March 1943, the Wehrmacht was still the dominant force in Europe and had yet to suffer catastrophic defeats in Tunisia and at Kursk in Russia. After these defeats, the Allies would seek unconditional surrender.

The third serious attempt on Hitler's life was at Rastenburg. On July 20, 1944, Claus von Stauffenberg, a disillusioned staff officer, left a bomb under the operations table at Hitler's headquarters. Miraculously, Hitler survived. However, this attempt was made so late in the war that even had it succeeded, German military fortunes could not be revived. Operation Bagration on the Eastern Front had all but wiped out Army Group Centre, and the Western Allies were poised to break out of their Normandy bridgehead.

The July plot's real consequence was that it allowed Hitler to clear out any resistance cells in the armed forces and Abwehr (German intelligence bureau). Hundreds died horribly, suspended from meat hooks, shot by firing squad, or beaten to death. Hitler had home movies of these slow, agonizing deaths and enjoyed watching them, late in the evening, as the thousand-year Reich tumbled around him.

One last attempt on the Führer's life was almost made after he had moved into the Berlin Bunker in 1945. His armaments minister, Albert Speer, realized that Hitler was determined to destroy Germany. According to Speer, he decided to save what he could and sought to obtain poison gas that he could pump into the bunker interior. Speer's attempt failed when extra security was placed at the bunker ventilators.

ABOVE **Hitler before the assassination attempt at Wolf's Lair. Claus Schenk Count von Stauffenberg is on the left.**

A Palpable Hit

Many people dislike lawyers, but it is a little-known fact that Vladimir Lenin graduated as a lawyer before going on to become a Marxist revolutionary. It was perhaps this training that allowed him to found the first modern totalitarian state, which became the inspiration for all subsequent dictators, including Hitler, Mao, and Stalin.

A desperate assassination attempt by Fanny Kaplan to stop the Bolsheviks seizing autocratic power led to an outbreak of violence never before seen in modern history.

Vladimir Ilyich Ulyanov was born on April 22, 1870, to a middle-class family in the heart of Russia and graduated as a lawyer in 1891. Like many intellectuals of the time, he was dissatisfied with the ancient autocratic system that ruled over Russia, but this became a burning hatred of the regime when his brother was executed for revolutionary activities. This hatred was exacerbated when Lenin was sentenced to several stints in captivity in Siberia, followed by a lengthy period of exile in Europe. During this time, from 1900, he began to develop Leninism, a radical adaption from the writings of Marx. While Marx envisaged communism developing from a capitalist/bourgeoisie society, Lenin wanted Russia to move from the semi-feudal state it was in under the Romanovs directly to a dictatorship of the proletariat.

With a stroke of his ideological pen, Lenin doomed millions of middle-class businessmen, farmers, and intelligentsia to ruthless extermination. When the 300-year-old

Romanov dynasty was overthrown in February 1917, Lenin returned to Russia and immediately began calling for a true revolution. This was achieved in October, with Lenin acting as the ideological head of the new regime and Trotsky organizing the military takeover. Once the ideologue gained power, he initiated his radical program to create a classless society. Banks were seized, industry was nationalized, other political parties were banned, the press was controlled, and laws were passed persecuting millions of members of the upper and middle classes.

Lenin's agenda outraged millions of Russians, including the Ukrainian anarchist Fanny Kaplan. She was at the heart of a conspiracy to destroy Lenin. On August 30, 1918, Lenin was leaving after making a speech to some Moscow workers and was about to enter his car when he was approached by a group of women. One of these seemed to usher the workers away from Lenin while Kaplan drew a revolver and shot Lenin twice. One bullet hit him in the left shoulder blade while the other lodged in the base of his neck, dangerously close to his vertebrae. She fired another shot but this ripped through his coat and hit one of his colleagues in the elbow.

Lenin was nothing if not tough, and he demanded to be taken to Bolshevik headquarters rather than a nearby hospital. He walked some of the way, even though he was bleeding profusely. Several hours later, surgeons arrived at the headquarters but did not operate on the second bullet for fear of paralyzing or killing Lenin. From this time on, Lenin was in almost constant pain, could not sleep, and suffered from blinding headaches. The bullets may have contributed to a series of strokes, the first in May 1922, and to his premature death on January 21, 1924, at the age of 53.

LEFT **Vladimir Lenin believed that the Russian Bourgeoisie had to be eliminated. The attempt on his life led to brutal class warfare.**

Fanny Kaplan met her fate a lot earlier—she was executed three days after the assassination attempt. After giving a full and somewhat suspect confession (she claimed that she alone was responsible for the shooting) to the Soviet secret police, the Cheka, she was escorted into a garage and executed with a single bullet to the back of the head. Her corpse was tossed into a barrel and set alight after petrol had been poured over it. Her remains were disposed of in an unknown location. Her death was organized by Yakov Sverdlov, who had ordered the execution of the royal family.

ABOVE **Fanny Kaplan may not have been the only shooter who attempted to take Lenin's life on August 30, 1918.**

She might have considered herself fortunate compared to others deemed to be enemies of the new regime. On the same day that the attempt was made on Lenin, the Petrograd Cheka boss was assassinated. This gave the Bolsheviks the opportunity to begin a monstrous act unparalleled in human history. On September 5, 1918, the decree on "Red Terror" was passed, which allowed the Cheka to seek to destroy a whole class, the Russian bourgeoisie (middle and upper classes). Whether it was the assassination attempts on Lenin that were responsible for spawning the Red Terror is open for debate.

They Shoot Like Pigs

Charles de Gaulle and his wife were proceeding through the streets of Paris on August 22, 1962, in his regular unarmored Citroën sedan. A team of 12 assassins opened up on the French president and sprayed the vehicle with several magazines of submachine gun bullets. Fourteen bullets hit the car, 20 hit a cafe behind the target, and another 187 hit the pavement and road around the chauffeur-driven sedan. Two motorcycle outriders died in the hail of gunfire and all four tires were shot out. Nevertheless, the superior suspension of the Citroën DS 19 allowed the chauffeur, De Gaulle, and his entourage to escape unscathed. De Gaulle proclaimed: "They shoot like pigs."

The French president entered the Guinness Book of Records as the political figure who had escaped the most assassination attempts at the time, 31 in all. This achievement could be put down to good luck but was more likely caused by his attackers' appalling lack of shooting skill.

Charles de Gaulle was born on November 22, 1890, in Lille, France. A fierce French patriot, he served with distinction at Verdun in World War I, and in World War II led an armored division in the six-week campaign in 1940 against German invasion, achieving some local successes. However, it was after the French surrender that he became an international figure. Refusing to lie supine under the German jackboot, he raised and led the Free French, a government in exile in opposition to the collaborationist Vichy regime. When France was liberated in 1944, De Gaulle was a national hero and began a long and successful political career.

However, despite his fierce French patriotism, De Gaulle was forced to witness the gradual roll back of France's colonial empire. In 1954, they quit Vietnam. In the same year, a fierce civil war broke out in Algeria, and the Organisation de L'Armée Secrète (OAS)

LEFT **Charles de Gaulle was a divisive figure in French society. He seemed to be loved and hated in equal measure.**

ABOVE **Charles de Gaulle survived many assassination attempts while driving in his favorite Citroën DS 19.**

was determined that this country would not leave the French empire. Elected to office, De Gaulle saw that further military expenditure to suppress the savage revolt would be futile and arranged for a three-year ceasefire to be followed by a referendum on independence in Algeria. The OAS saw this as an admission of defeat and began a ruthless campaign to kill the president.

So many attempts were made on De Gaulle's life that he and his wife became almost blasé. He continued to ride in his unarmored Citroën, and when the car was again sprayed with bullets in August 1962, he and his wife refused to take cover. After the attempt, he calmly brushed the broken glass off his sleeve.

This unflappable calm saved De Gaulle several more times. Even before these attempts on September 8, 1961, the OAS detonated a roadside bomb made up of 110 pounds (50 kilos) of plastic explosive and 4 US gallons (15 liters) of napalm as the president approached his country home. The car was almost blown off the road but the president calmly ordered his chauffeur to keep driving through the flames, and the car and its occupants emerged safe and sound.

On November 9, 1970, De Gaulle dropped dead of a ruptured blood vessel in his neck, two weeks short of his 80th birthday.

THE LUCKIEST MAN TO HAVE LIVED?

In 1959, Fidel Castro seized power in Cuba. The setting up of a Stalinist state within shooting distance of America was like a red rag to a bull. The Americans were determined to get rid of the red dictator and played around with many crazy methods to eliminate him. These ranged from depilatory cream to full-scale armed invasion.

Different methods discussed or even attempted included poisoning his chocolate milkshake; a drive-by shooting by a Mafia hit man; a grenade attack at a sporting event; placing several pounds (kilograms) of explosive under a podium where he was to speak; a garishly colored explosive conch shell to be placed where he would find it while swimming; covering a hankie with deadly germs; a ballpoint pen hypodermic syringe filled with toxins; and, most famously, an exploding cigar.

Many of the most bizarre methods intended to kill Castro came from the American Central Intelligence Agency (CIA). But while the KGB was developing extremely effective methods of assassinating political opponents, most of the CIA attempts seemed more like something from a Monty Python script.

BELOW **Fidel Castro survived a CIA attempt to plant explosives in his cigar. He gave up smoking in 1985.**

ABOVE Fidel Castro and his brother Raul Castro survived multiple assassination attempts sponsored by the CIA, the Mafia, and Cuban exiles.

The CIA decided that if it was too difficult to kill Castro, they could discredit him. Castro made regular speeches from a media booth, and the Americans planned to spray the interior with LSD. It was hoped that this would make him talk nonsense, thus losing respect in the Cuban community. A similar attempt was made to lace a box of his favorite cigars with a hallucinogenic. Another CIA boffin came up with a scheme to lace his cigars with a depilatory agent, thus causing the dictator's beard to fall out. A box of cigars was treated with the lethal toxin botulinum; so deadly were these cigars that he only had to place one between his lips to receive a deadly dose. For various reasons, all these schemes went up in smoke. Undeterred, an attempt was made to put thallium powder in Castro's shoes. This too was intended to make his beard fall out and convert the strongman into a laughing stock.

Castro gave up smoking in 1985 and, like all good dictators, never advertised his whereabouts while maintaining a network of at least 20 residences throughout Cuba. He died peacefully in Havana on November 25, 2016.

A BOX OF CIGARS WAS TREATED WITH THE LETHAL TOXIN BOTULINUM; SO DEADLY WERE THESE CIGARS THAT HE ONLY HAD TO PLACE ONE BETWEEN HIS LIPS TO RECEIVE A DEADLY DOSE.

Wannabe Taxi Driver

Many American presidents have survived assassination attempts. Andrew Jackson, Theodore Roosevelt, Franklin D. Roosevelt, Harry S. Truman, and Gerald Ford all survived planned attempts to change the political landscape.

Ronald Reagan narrowly escaped an attempt in 1981. Given his strident anti-Communist rhetoric, it might be expected that his attacker was a Soviet agent trained for years in KGB assassination attempts. Not so. A hopeless deranged drifter named John W. Hinckley got through layers of security and almost took down the most powerful man in the world.

The US Secret Service (USSS) was founded in 1865 and after the assassination of William McKinley in 1901 was given the responsibility of protecting the president. The initial deployment was two agents attached full time to the White House, but over the years the security detachment has grown exponentially, as has the number of people it has to protect. The president's family, the vice president and the president's relatives, as well as all past incumbents, now merit their own security detail. (Children of past presidents are given security details until they turn 16!) With the terrorist threat of the new millennium, this branch of government now has more than 6,000 staff with approximately 3,000 special agents. They are the frontline security experts and can usually be recognized by their sunglasses, earphone comms, and a distinctive oval-shaped badge on their left lapel.

It was fortunate for President Reagan that he was surrounded by a professional detail, and one agent even took a bullet for "Rawhide" Reagan, as he was known by the USSS operatives. So good was this protection that Reagan didn't even realize he had been hit when one of Hinckley's bullets ricocheted off his arm bone into his lung.

On March 30, 1981, Reagan had given a speech at the Washington Hilton and was walking to the presidential limousine when he was shot (strangely, only seven days earlier Reagan had visited the Ford Theater in Washington where Lincoln was shot and had felt a tingling up his spine as he looked into the Lincolns' box). He was usually advised by his Secret Service operatives to wear a bulletproof vest, but for once he refused, deciding that the short walk from the lecture venue to the car was only 30 feet (9 meters) and that there could not possibly be a threat. Another sign of the innocence of the times was the Presidential Press Office releasing an itinerary for the president's movements that day. It is unlikely that such information would be made available today.

Reagan, like many other Republican presidents before and after his tenure, was anti-gun control. The Second Amendment guarantees all Americans the right to bear arms. This allows any number of crackpots, madmen, survivalists, criminals, and killers to get their hands on huge arsenals of handguns, shotguns, semiautomatics, and automatic weaponry.

John W. Hinckley, born May 29, 1955, is a prime example of an individual with many personality disorders who, despite giving many warning signs, was able to amass an arsenal of weapons. Hinckley was obsessed with the actress Jodie Foster, and after watching her feature film *Taxi Driver* he hatched the plan to kill the president. A similar plot is contained in the movie, and Hinckley's warped reality led him to believe that by killing Reagan he would earn Foster's affections.

Hinckley came from a prosperous background but from an early age displayed disturbing tendencies and an explosive temper. He joined the National Socialist Party (the American Nazi party) but was expelled in less than a year for his extremist views. Two years later, in 1980, he was arrested at Nashville Airport for trying to carry on board three

BELOW President Ronald Reagan provoked the USSR with his anti-Soviet "Evil Empire" sentiments. However, it was a deranged American who almost killed him.

ABOVE **President Ronald Reagan waves as he leaves the Washington, DC, Hilton seconds before being shot by John Hinckley, Jr.**

guns combined with several boxes of ammunition. Jimmy Carter was in Nashville that day, and it was likely that he would have been Hinckley's first target. The clearly unbalanced would-be assassin received a slap on the wrist in the form of a small fine. No further action was taken and as soon as Hinckley was released by the Tennessee authorities he purchased another handgun, a Röhm RG-14 .22 LR. His choice of weapon showed that Hinckley wasn't totally deranged but was planning his assassination attempt well. The Röhm is a tiny .22 caliber pistol with a small handgrip and snub barrel, perfect for concealment in even one hand. What's more, Hinckley had loaded the gun with six "Devastator" cartridges, designed to explode on contact. During the attack, only one exploded.

This weapon's only weakness is its lack of stopping power—a successful hit requires all six rounds to impact the target. Hinckley managed to get off all six shots but, fortunately for Reagan, only one hit him.

The Secret Service had screened those who attended the president's speech, but as he exited the hotel and approached his limousine there was a large crowd of admirers roped off from his route. The president stopped to wave at the crowd, who were less than 15 feet (4.5 meters) away, and Hinckley took his chance. In 1.7 seconds, he squeezed off all six shots. The first bullet hit press secretary James Brady in the head, a wound that would kill him years later. A local police officer was then hit in the back of the neck. The third shot passed above Reagan while the fourth bullet hit special agent Timothy McCarthy as he leapt between Reagan and the shooter. The fifth and sixth bullets hit the armored limousine, and one of them ricocheted off the vehicle and passed through the target's left underarm and through his ribs to lodge in a lung, less than 1 inch (2.5 cm) from his heart. Special agent Parr had shoved Reagan into the limousine, and the president thought the pain in his chest was from Parr's rough shove.

Hinckley was wrestled to the ground by several bystanders and local police as the gun fell from his hand. As Reagan and his guard sped off in the presidential limousine, it was thought that he only had cracked ribs, but things got a lot more serious when the president started coughing up bright, frothy blood.

Keeping up his he-man image, Reagan managed to walk unaided through the foyer of George Washington University Hospital but collapsed as he entered the emergency wing, complaining of difficulty breathing and lack of balance. His blood pressure plummeted, and it was only due to his overall good health that he managed to pull through. It was only confirmed that he had been shot when the surgeon found the bullet's tiny entry wound.

Reagan maintained his cheerful persona, wisecracking to his wife, Nancy, "Honey, I forgot to duck," and passing a note to a nurse saying "All in all, I'd rather be in Philadelphia." A classic W.C. Fields line.

Reagan was operated on, and during this surgery he lost more than half his blood before the bleeding could be contained. After almost two hours under the knife, the bullet was finally removed. But Reagan's problems were not over. Post-operative infections set in, causing difficulty breathing or focusing for many months afterward. Nevertheless, the president had won office on a platform of making the USA great again and staring down the Soviet "Evil Empire," and as a result he had to maintain the illusion that he was virtually untouched by the attack.

This may have contributed to Hinckley receiving a verdict of not guilty due to insanity at his trial on June 21, 1982. This prompted a public outcry at the leniency of the sentence and led to several changes making it harder to prove insanity in federal courts.

The attack may have sped up Reagan's Alzheimer's disease, and by the time his second term came to an end there was evidence that he was failing to comprehend the day-to-day requirements of his position. He finally died at the age of 93 in his Californian Bel Air home on June 5, 2004.

Hinckley was released in September 2016 after 35 years of psychiatric treatment and moved in with his 90-year-old mother in Williamsburg, Virginia.

Pope John Paul II

It seems that God, if there is one, looked after Pope John Paul II. He survived both the Nazi and the Communist regimes to become head of the Catholic Church for 27 years and then survived several assassination attempts.

John Paul was born Karol Josef Wojtyla in Wadowice, Poland, on May 18, 1920. He was brought up in a very religious household where his mother doted on the young boy and was convinced that he would do great things. His father was an army officer, and when the Nazis invaded Poland the two fled to the east, only to find that the Soviets had occupied the eastern half of their country. They returned to Krakow where Josef had been studying and tried their best to survive under the Nazi jack-boot. Prior to the war, Josef had excelled at Krakow University, becoming fluent in many languages.

During the occupation, he flirted with danger and joined the Resistance, where he helped Jews escape to the east. He was hit by a tram during this time before being accidently run over by a German truck, which led to permanent damage to his posture. This was a near-death experience for the young man and convinced him to join the priesthood after the war.

Karol Josef began training for the priesthood in an underground seminary. He escaped several Nazi round-ups during the Warsaw uprising, which had spread to other major towns, including Krakow. Eight thousand young men were hauled off but Karol Josef was more fortunate and managed to hide in his uncle's basement before escaping to the local archbishop's residence. His mother and two siblings had died before the war, and in 1941 his father died, leaving Karol as the last surviving member of his family.

The young man was ordained in 1946 and began his rapid rise through the Church hierarchy, becoming the youngest bishop in Poland in 1958, Archbishop of Krakow in 1964, and a cardinal in 1967. In August 1978, he was ordained as Pope John Paul II.

Seen as one of the good popes, John Paul used his position to oppose apartheid in South Africa and argued against the use of capital punishment. He also opposed the Gulf War in 1991 and was the first pope to use his moral authority to argue against the Mafia.

In 1983, the Soviets tried character assassination against the pope, attempting to prove that he had fathered an illegitimate child; but a much more serious attempt to kill him had been made two years earlier.

On the afternoon of May 13, 1981, the pope entered St Peter's square to a rapturous welcome from some 10,000 eager pilgrims. As his open-topped white vehicle drove slowly through the square, a hand emerged from the crowd and fired several shots from a pistol, a lethal 9mm Browning semiautomatic. At least two bullets tore into the pope, striking his hand and tearing into his innards. The stricken prelate was immediately rushed to intensive care at Gemelli Hospital, where it took six hours of surgery to stop catastrophic bleeding from the multiple wounds inflicted by the would-be assassin. Particularly dangerous was one bullet lodged in his lower intestine.

As soon as the pistol discharged, the attacker fled through the stunned crowd, but was wrestled to the ground by enraged pilgrims, the pope's head of security, and a nun. The would-be assassin turned out to be a mentally unstable Turkish self-proclaimed terrorist named Mehmet Ali Agca. He had a particularly murky past and was associated with the Grey Wolves, a far-right Turkish terrorist group, the PLA (Palestinian Liberation Army), the Bulgarian secret police, and the Russian KGB. Ali Agca was sentenced to life imprisonment but was released by Italian authorities when Pope John Paul publicly forgave him and called for him to be pardoned.

It is likely that the KGB connection is the most realistic reason for the assassination attempt. The Soviet leader Yuri Andropov was concerned with the pope's interference with Polish domestic politics and in particular his support for the Solidarity movement.

John Paul survived several other attempts, including one by a Portuguese priest, Juan María Fernández y Krohn, who was convinced the pope was a Soviet agent. He tried to stab the pope with a bayonet but was only sentenced to six years' incarceration.

BELOW Pope John Paul II speaks with his attacker. The Pope made it clear that he forgave Mehmet Ali Agca.

Further Reading

Books

Ascher, Abraham. P.A. Stolypin: *The Search for Stability in Late Imperial Russia*. Stanford, CA, Stanford University Press, 2001.

Davis, Lee. *Assassination: Twenty Assassinations that Changed History*. London, Transedition Books, 1993.

Durden Smith, Jo. *100 Most Infamous Criminals*. London, Arcturus Publishing, 2003.

Greig, Charlotte. *Cold-Blooded Killings: Hits, Assassinations and Near Misses that Shook the World*. London, Arcturus Publishing, 2006.

Hartley, Janet. *Profiles in Power: Alexander I. Harlow*, Essex, UK, Longman, 1994.

Jacobs, David H. *The Mafia's Greatest Hits*. New York, Kensington Publishing, 2006.

Malone, Richard. *Analysing the Russian Revolution*. Cambridge, UK, Cambridge University Press, 2015.

Perfect, Lauren, Ryan, Tom and Sweeney, Scott. *Reinventing Russia: The Revolutionary Experience*. Collingwood, VA, History Teachers' Association of Victoria, 2008.

Pollock, Alan. *Vietnam Conflict and Change in Indochina*. Oxford, UK, Oxford University Press, 1998.

Pyes, Craig, and Rempel, William C. "Slowly Stalking an Afghan 'Lion'". *LA Times*, June 2002.

Summerscale, Kate. *The Wicked Boy: The Mystery of a Victorian Child Murderer*. London, Bloomsbury, 2016.

Sutterman, H.S. *Crimes and Punishment: The Illustrated Crime Encyclopaedia*. Connecticut, Marshall Cavendish, 1994.

Warnes, David. *Chronicle of the Russian Tsars*. London, Thames and Hudson, 1999.

Websites

American Mafia History
http://americanmafiahistory.com

Biography
www.biography.com

JFK Lancer
www.jfklancer.com

J-Grit: The Internet Index of Tough Jews
www.j-grit.com

saint-petersburg.com
www.saint-petersburg.com

Vanity Fair
www.vanityfair.com

INDEX

Page numbers in **bold** refer to captions.

E

F

G

H

I

J

K

Picture Credits

3 © Morphart Creation | Shutterstock • 4 © linea | Shutterstock • 5 © De Luan | Alamy Stock Photo • 8 © Asavaa | Creative Commons • 10, 35, 43, 68, 109, 110, 194, 196 © Wellcome Image Library • 12, 56 © Dorotheum | Creative Commons • 14 © Museum Crozatier | Shutterstock • 16 © Chronicle | Alamy Stock Photo • 18 © Lebrecht Music and Arts Photo Library | Alamy Stock Photo • 19 © Rlbberlin | Creative Commons • 21 © Marie-Lan Nguyen | Creative Commons • 23 © World History Archive | Alamy Stock Photo • 24 © Curioso | Shutterstock • 26 © DEA | G. Dagli Orti | De Agostini | Getty Images • 27 © Brigida Soriano | Shutterstock • 28 © kladcat | Creative Commons • 30, 42 © Classic Image | Alamy Stock Photo • 33 © Georgios Kolidas | Shutterstock • 34 © 19th era | Alamy StockPhoto • 48 © Chronicle | Alamy Stock Photo • 49 © Bjoertvedt | Creative Commons • 50 © Lebrecht Music and Arts Photo Library | Alamy Stock Photo • 60 © Csh012 | Creative Commons • 64 © Heritage Image Partnership Ltd | Alamy Stock Photo • 66 © Leemage | UIG via Getty Images • 76 © Granbergs Konstindustri Aktiebolags Förlag • 81 © Malcolm Browne | Creative Commons • 86, 123, 128, 174 © Everett Historical Collection | Alamy Stock Photo • 92 © Yann | Creative Commons • 94 © DR Travel Photo and Video | Shutterstock • 100 © Barry Iverson | Alamy Stock Photo • 106 © ART Collection | Alamy Stock Photo • 107 fonte | Creative Commons • 114 © Fullangel1 | Creative Commons • 118 © Éclusette | Creative Commons • 119 © Apic | Getty Images • 121 © Askild Antonsen | Creative Commons • 130, 132, 187, 217 © Bettmann | Getty Images • 133 © wasanajai | Shutterstock • 135 © Photo 12 | Alamy Stock Photo • 136 © Ricardo Stuckert | PR | Agencia Brasil | Creative Commons • 138 © mrlopez2681 | Creative Commons • 141 © Wojtek Laski | Getty Images • 143, 146, 147, 197 © Everett Historical | Shutterstock • 149 © Francisco Peralta Torrejon | Creative Commons • 150, 200, 201 © ullstein bild | Getty Images • 152 © Terence Spencer | The LIFE Images Collection | Getty Images • 153 © Tanja Kragujevic | Creative Commons • 154 © Slavko Sereda | Shutterstock • 156, 158 © Moviestore collection Ltd | Alamy Stock Photo • 157 © Maurizio Pesce | Creative Commons • 160 © Joost Evers | Anefo | Creative Commons • 163 © Mug Shot | Alamy Stock Photo • 164 © P.Lindgren | Creative Commons • 165 © Чигот | Creative Commons • 166 © pcruciatti | Creative Commons • 167 © travelview | Shutterstock • 168 © Victor Watts | Alamy Stock Photo • 172 © Ed Giorandino | NY Daily News via Getty Images • 175 © EQRoy | Shutterstock • 176, 179 © Granger Historical Picture Archive | Alamy Stock Photo • 181 © Janelle Lugge | Shutterstock • 183 © New York Police Department | Shutterstock • 184 © New York Times Co. | Hulton Archive | Getty Images • 185 © Mary DiBiase | NY Daily News Archive via Getty Images • 188 © Thomas Monaster | NY Daily News Archive via Getty Images • 191 © Enzo Brai | Mondadori Portfolio via Getty Images • 199 © Heinrich Hoffmann | ullstein bild via Getty Images • 203 © Artenex | Shutterstock • 204 © IgorGolovniov | Shutterstock • 207 © SPUTNIK | Alamy Stock Photo • 208 © Bibliotheque National de France • 209 © Gnotype | Creative Commons • 210 © David Hume Kennerly | Getty Images • 214 © CORBIS | Corbis via Getty Images

All other images in this book are in the public domain.

Every effort has been made to credit the copyright holders of the images used in this book. We apologize for any unintentional omissions or errors, and will insert the appropriate acknowledgement to any companies or individuals in subsequent editions of the work.